The Worldly Spirit And The Inside Seal

By Father Spyridon Turnea

Translated from romanian language by Vasilescu Ruxandra and Camelia Frunza
Revised by Aliki Los, second revision by Father Jacobs and Daniel Wilkinson

According to ancient tradition, a third of the angels fell, following Satan. *"His tail drew a third of the stars of heaven and threw them to the earth"* (Revelation 12, 4). How was this possible? Why are so few people saints? Is any connection between the angels' fall and man's fall? What kind of spirit blows in the soul in those moments?

The book is an Orthodox answer to these questions. The Ancient Fathers come to illuminate this mystery, to show the connection between the fall of the angels and the fall of man.

Saint John of Kronstadt stated: "If you don't know the worldly spirit, you won't know the life-giving Spirit either." You can't talk about the Holy Spirit if you don't first understand the worldly spirit. The spirit of worldly vanity...

.

Contents

Chapter 5

The Inner Seal

Chapter 1

The Spirit of Worldly Vanity

The Beginning

I remember that once, while returning from the market, I saw a young woman getting out of a car. At that moment, I felt such disgust for her state of happiness and fulfillment that I had to think about it for a long time.

First, I thought that it was envy, I was being judgmental, or something like that. But, no, I would not have wanted to own that car or been in the state that she was, because I was feeling disgust.

The car, though, was not luxurious; I could not say that I was disgusted by luxury or by the young woman appearing indecent. On the contrary, she was dressed decently, even unadorned, and she was not wearing make-up. She looked like a young college graduate, the child whom many parents would like to have.

I realized that I was disgusted by her delight in her material things and by the fact that she looked satiated and full and seemed to say with the rich man in the Gospel: "*Soul, you have many goods laid up for many years; take your ease; eat, drink and be merry*" (Luke 12:19). Although this woman didn't look rich, she seemed very delighted with the things that she had and with what she was.

I was confused about why I did not admire such people, and I thought about that occurrence for a long while. Some time later, I found myself in front of a dying man; I was rejoicing that he no longer wanted to rejoice in any earthly things, when his soul seemed to reject them and look for something else.

My two attitudes seemed unnatural, and I sought an answer. I was ready to admit any mistake, but I first had to know where I might have been wrong. Should I have shared the young woman's happiness because she seemed to have a satisfying, successful life? Should I have grieved that the dying man could no longer enjoy delicious food or a vacation or watching TV for the latest sports scores?

I studied these questions with the utmost attention.

Broken Cisterns

Driven by these concerns, I started to write. After a while, I noticed that the good state I felt in Church during Sunday religious services disappeared in a few hours. Or, more accurately, it began to disappear within five or ten minutes or sometimes almost immediately after coming out of the church. All the power that seemed to fill my soul in church or when reading an akathist vanished completely. The world was again attracting me; my free will seemed to once again become feeble and unable to oppose the stream of the world dragging me into its rush. For my state of spiritual peace to disappear, I only had to turn on the TV, or meet an acquaintance for a talk, or pass by a place where worldly music was playing, or hear a joke. ... Even going to work and interacting with my colleagues or relatives could fill me again with "something else" different from that which filled my soul during prayer or attending church.

I came across discussions about grace and wondered whether I could also receive it in the Church. From various books, I found out how grace works in the Church and how believers receive it through the Church Sacraments. I was convinced that it is true because I had felt it, too, somehow. However, what seems very important to me is not how we receive grace **but how we lose it**.

A layman might lose grace in thousands of ways, I found out. I think this is why it is extremely rare for Orthodox Christians to reach home after the Sunday Divine Liturgy without losing grace. If they have the TV on, grace is ousted in a few seconds or minutes. This can also happen when someone browses newspapers, accesses the Internet, or in many other situations. Disquiet replaces the peace of heart which bears witness to the presence of grace. The lust for business, the desire to see worldly things, or a combination of all these, again draws the Christian into the same stream he got out of during prayer.

I have done my best to learn exactly when grace leaves me. I repeat: it was very, very important for me to know how the grace which we attain through the Holy Sacraments and Church services is lost. Otherwise, Christians cannot spiritually grow, even if they go to Church regularly and are active members of the Church. Christians lose grace as regularly as they receive it.

Knowing how we receive grace is as important as knowing how we lose it so that we not waste it but, instead, help it grow and bear fruit in our souls. Otherwise, we will always be in an immature, fruitless state, ignoring or even fighting against the true Orthodoxy.

Consider the following example: let us assume that a man gives us a coin, but because our pocket has a hole, the coin falls out. Arriving home, we see that we do not have it any more, so we run back to get another coin. And that good man, full of benevolence, gives us one more coin, which we lose in the same way. After many years, what will be the use of much money passing through our hands if we end up without anything?! Some people might choose to defame the very person who has given them the money, calling him a deceiver. They might even hit or kill that man, claiming that he caused them to waste their time in vain!

The coin, though, was real; you held it in your hands for a moment and saw that it was good. But now, you no longer have it. After experiencing this over and over again, it would be appropriate to investigate whether there is a way to not lose the money, for the grace received in the soul to not be lost but to grow and bear fruit.

Otherwise, the state of continued scatterings of grace can lead us to a state of perplexity, unbelief, or revolt against God. Such states can increasingly be seen all around us: the Church and the Sacraments seem to have lost their power. Nevertheless, grace is the same; we simply don't know how to preserve it.

Some have considered the administration of the Holy Sacraments to be a solution, requiring no other measures, but that is like asking for more money without repairing the hole in your pocket. As Saint John Chrysostom said, those who were worthy of Baptism and rejoiced in the Holy Sacraments will be utterly useless unless they prove that they can live lives worthy of the grace received. No matter how much money you receive and put in your torn pocket, it will be lost if you are not careful to patch the holes through which it slips. This is the work of the foolish virgins, who didn't have the grace of the Holy Spirit in their lamps, as explained by Saint Seraphim of Sarov: "I think that what they were lacking was the grace of the All-Holy Spirit of God. These virgins practiced the virtues, but in their spiritual ignorance, they assumed that the Christian life consisted merely of doing good works. By doing a good deed they thought they were doing the work of God, but they cared little whether they acquired the grace of God's Spirit. Such ways of life based merely on doing good without carefully testing whether it brings the grace of the Spirit of God, are mentioned in the Patristic books: There is another way which is deemed good at the beginning, but it ends at the bottom of hell."

The foolish virgins do not only exist in the Savior's example; they are real and in great number in the Orthodox Church. The Prophet Jeremiah says something similar: "*For My people have committed two evils: They have forsaken Me, the fountain of living waters, and hewn themselves cisterns -**broken cistern**s that can hold no water*" (Jeremiah 2:13).

When I studied the writings of the Saints, it all started to clear up. Here is what Saint John Chrysostom says: "you may fall after two days and lose the name of newly illuminated (newly baptized) and grace". "Now often the highest grace of the Holy Spirit flies away from the most hardened sinners".

Also, Saint John of Kronstadt says: "in the hearts of those who do not pray, the seeds of every evil grow, smothering the small amount of good that has remained in them from the grace of baptism, chrism, and subsequent penitence, and Holy Communion".

And in other place Saint John of Kronstadt says: "you must refrain from attachments to earthly things, and from impure risings of the flesh; otherwise, **the priceless treasure of the Holy Spirit will immediately leave you**, peace and joy will vanish from your heart together with that feeling of the extraordinary, angelic, spiritual lightness of the soul, soaring free; the rivers of living water, which only until then flowed and abundantly supplied the furrows of the soul, will also vanish".

As a layman involved in numerous problems concerning the company, family, and job, I thought that grace could only be in my heart rarely and faintly. I had to recognize that I was actually serving mammon, as my mind was full of plans and projects to make money, and the Gospel clearly says: *You cannot serve God and mammon.* (Matthew 6: 24)

Often, in my heart, there has seemed to be "something else" which gives me life, animates me, entertains me, makes me clap my hands in happiness. Just like in the case of grace, I sometimes feel this "something else" strongly in my heart, but at other times, it seems to disappear. My heart thirsts powerfully for this "something else"; rather, it has been incited to thirst after this "something else". It has seemed to me that it is wonderful to have my heart filled with this "something else". Other people besides me also seem to run after this "something else".

I have noticed that my heart fills with this "something else" when I am sitting at the tavern drinking and chatting about my favorite team's wins, listening to jokes or music, or watching TV. My heart also fills with this "something else" when I receive praise or daydream and in many other situations.

I began to notice that the grace I felt from church vanished when my heart filled with this "something else". I was amazed, and moreover, due to God's care I found books written by the saints of the Church which revealed these same things. In particular, the book *About Delusion* by Saint Ignatius Brianchaninov was very useful to me, but also other books by the Holy Fathers.

However, I found it more difficult to notice when exactly grace was leaving me, and easier to notice when my heart was filling with this "something else". It was difficult for me to notice when grace was leaving me because I had very little experience with grace, but plenty of experience with this "something else". We are born, grown up, imbued and immersed in this "something else"; therefore I could observe it much more clearly when it was filling my soul. When it appeared, I knew for sure that the received grace had gone or was about to go away, unless I could quickly snatch myself away from this "something else".

But what exactly was that "something else" that I was being filled with? It concerned me for a long time. In time, I found many definitions and important ideas about that "something else" which surrounds us, even since birth.

Saint Theophan the Recluse says the following about it: "A sort of curtain of darkness, a smoke – I tell you – seems to have been unleashed upon the heart, which gets out of the fire of the spirit of the world, which hinders the thought itself to communicate with God, and the soul to pray by its own will or to believe or love God". Then he specifies: "**One cannot live without the spirit of life; whoever lives is necessarily animated by something**. The appropriate spirit of the

Christian is the spirit of Christ, which should animate us, subduing to its dominion all the rest and making them its ministering tools. The spirit of Christ resides in doing everything to God's glory and our own salvation.

The opposite of the spirit of Christ **is the spirit of the world, at whose command people, forgetting about God, work without getting tired, and run in vain, to chase deceptive goals** which they never seem to achieve; and if they do, they never enjoy the peace of having fulfilled their goals. It is also called a *delusive spirit,* which under various nice appearances attracts a lot of people, taking the form of a bright angel". And somewhere else, he adds: "Those who believe in God fill with a completely different spirit, averse to the spirit which possessed people before its coming".

"True Christianity will become weaker and weaker, and finally will vanish; the only thing that will remain will be the name Christian, but there won't be any Christian spirit. **The spirit of the world fills everything**".

"He who will breathe unto himself just a little bit of the spirit of the world will become distant towards Christianity and to its teachings. The spirit of the world with all the teachings harmful to the soul accompanying it, is a spirit adverse to Christ, it is the spirit of the Antichrist; its spreading means the spreading of hatred over Christian belief and the Christian ordinances of life. It seems that around us, things are going this way … **The spirit of the Antichrist is always the same; what was at the beginning will also be now, perhaps under a different form, but with the same meaning**".

We are born, raised, surrounded and immersed in this spirit of deception, the spirit of worldly vanity, which strives to replace the grace in our human heart just like the Antichrist will strive to replace Christ. It also offers a sort of joy and a sort of life. It is familiar to all humans because it is the spirit which rules in the world, it is the spirit of the Antichrist. When the heart fills with this worldly spirit, grace leaves us. Or even if grace does not leave us, then it sorrows, and we are about to lose it.

Also, Saint Ignatius Brianchaninov says in his book *About Delusion*: "Delusion is the wounding of the people souls by lie. Delusion is the state of all mankind, without any exception, and it started after the fall of our proto-parents. All of us are deluded. All of us are deceived. All of us are in a state of lie, and we need to be released and find out the Truth. And the Truth is our Lord Jesus Christ".

Saint Symeon the New Theologian says the true Christian "sees all things as they are by nature, and **does not marvel at their colors and brightness**". And Saint John Chrysostom says very clearly: "**Those who are amazed by the things of this life, they all walk through the wide door and the wide path**". In *Commentary on the Psalms* by Saint Basil the Great, he says: "Only a few people do not marvel at worldly things, although they all depend on God". Truly blessed is someone like this because he is not enraptured with earthly things like unto his own things, nor is he attached to the things from here as by a natural homeland".

Saint Tikhon of Zadonsk adds: "Oh, eternal life! How sweet and dear you are, but few are those who love you! Oh, world, world, valley of weeping! How bitter you are and yet almost everybody loves you! What would happen if you were sweet? No doubt, everybody would deem it as their homeland and a second heaven". "When this fear and longing leave the heart (longing for God), then the longing for this world dwells in it".

Balcony Painting – A Case Study

Once I painted my balcony with my own hands, and I was so delighted that day that I could not think of anything else. I felt a vain delight, which kept me enchained. I was looking again and again to see how well it turned out. I realized that I had to tear myself away, but I couldn't. I was pleased, delighted and fulfilled. A scornful thought arose in my mind: Why should I care about the Kingdom of Heaven when it is so good here? It was the first time that I had painted the balcony, and it turned out very well.

Fortunately for me, a few hours later, a heavy rain came pouring down and washed away a little of the fresh lime. I was no longer thinking of painting, and my heart was no longer stuck to the balcony. It now had a few spots. I regained my peace and my usual state. A short time after, I repainted it, but not completely. There were still a few spots left, but now everything was all right. I knew that it could be destroyed and that there was no point in filling my mind with vain delight. Thank God who once again saved me! His will be done in all things.

At first, I said to myself that I would rather never paint it again than to fill myself with that state. However, after a while, after a long delay when any delight I had vanished, I started repainting the balcony. No, there was no delight now. In other words, my soul was no longer being filled with the spirit of vanity and was no longer sticking to the work done.

We often hear: "This thing is full of delight!" or "there is no delight in doing this!" In most cases, it is about the vanity which is, or is not, filling our heart.

Let's be steadfast, let's take heed: *Those who rejoice should be as though they did not rejoice* (I Corinthians 7: 30).

God often delays in fulfilling our demands and waits for the time when we will no longer fill ourselves with delight and will no longer tie our hearts to that demanded thing. More often than not we receive something asked for when we seem not to enjoy it any longer; this is usually because of the long wait and feeling of unrest that precedes it. And this just means that the answer to our prayer came in its own time; a time when it does not endanger our salvation, through dangerous attachments to things, events, ways of life and people. It comes at the proper time to meet the Christian's demand, when his heart does not fill with vain amazement and when he will not attach himself to that thing or situation which would be an attachment to the world and worldly things. This is because worldly things are vain and quickly vanish. *"Those who weep as though they did not weep, those who rejoice as though they did not rejoice, those who buy as though they did not possess, and those who use this world as not misusing it..."* (I Corinthians 7:30)

Thus, if such desires were met quickly, we would get more and more attached to earthly things, to the devil's delight and God's sadness. This applies both in the case of materials things, and in the case of virtues. If you delight or attach yourself to a certain virtue and make it worldly by relating it to other people and to worldly things, then it will be taken away from you because it is not useful for your salvation. God gives us as many gifts as we can handle without filling ourselves with the spirit of worldly vanity.

How we Receive Grace

Saint Theophan the Recluse says: "We receive the grace of the Holy Spirit with the Holy Sacraments of Baptism and Chrismation. When participating in the divine cult of our Church, by faith, by prayers, by spiritual struggle and practicing virtues, **grace is preserved and works inside us**. A good way of attaining this purpose is the prayer of the heart, which attracts the Holy Spirit. Due to our faith in Christ, we become worthy of the grace".

Saint John of Kronstadt says that we acquire: "the grace of God in the Church, the Divine services, the Sacraments, our conscience, our inward trial and cleansing by God, prayers, the afflictions that cleanse our hearts, and also sicknesses. The soul is supported by prayer, by reading God's Word, and by the communion of The Holy Sacraments".

Saint Seraphim of Sarov adds to this other means whereby we can acquire it by listing almost all the traditional good deeds of lay Christians or monks: "Prayer, fasting, vigil, alms-giving, and all the other Christian practices serve as the indispensable means for the acquisition of the Holy Spirit of God".

However, it is not about how we receive it, preserve and multiply, but **about how we lose it**. Because when it is not lost, grace is growing, working, and multiplying. *"The Helper, the Holy Spirit, He will teach you all things"* (John 14:26). In other words, The Spirit of Truth leads us mysteriously. Saint John Chrysostom tells us what he leads us to: "This is the nature of grace, to snatch someone from earthly things and to raise him to heaven".

What is the Role of Grace?

Saint Silouan the Athonite says: "The Holy Spirit teaches the soul to fulfill God's commands and gives it the strength to do good."

Saint Theophan the Recluse says: "It is impossible for us to deny greed without the influence of grace upon the heart; it is impossible, without God's grace, to put an end to any other passion or sin living in ourselves and also with all the springs of these sins". And further: Without the grace of the Holy Spirit, we cannot become saints, martyrs, confessors or Christian zealots. And "So long as there is zeal, there is also the grace of the Holy Spirit". We may say that any attraction towards the Church and towards the narrow path, to follow the saints even nowadays, is proof that grace is working. The same Saint says: "Zeal is the work of grace and the proof that this grace is always present in yourselves, and it gives birth to the graceful life. So long as there is zeal, the grace of the Holy Spirit is present too".

Grace is the same in all Orthodox churches, we are told. But in some of them, there are many who work together with that grace and light, and they spread the rays of grace further, while in others, on the contrary, they refuse to work together with that grace and thus, remain dark, spreading nothing. In both cases, grace is the same, but the cooperation with it differs.

Saint Tikhon of Zadonsk says: "the grace of God is to the soul what the soul is for the body. So, just as the body is dead without the soul in it, the soul is dead when the life-giving grace of God is not in it". And further: "The sons of this century enjoy the honor, glory, gold, silver, wealth, delights and pleasures of this world. These are their treasure, consolation, and joy, and they enjoy this treasure of theirs because they love it. Christians must banish this joy away from their hearts and not make a dwelling for it therein. It is the joy which the Holy Spirit tells us to avoid: *"Do not love the world or the things in the world* (1 John: 2:15). Because, that which man loves, he enjoys, and, therefore Christians must not love the world or enjoy it".

Saint John Chrysostom says: "It is impossible for someone to endure martyrdom courageously, to preach zealously, or to achieve a great and difficult deed unless the power of the Holy Spirit strengthens and gives courage to the martyr. Otherwise, no one could be a martyr. And I refer to a martyr here as someone who has not only ended his life in suffering for Christ but who also confesses Christ with the word of grace. Any preacher of truth is a martyr for God. It is impossible to be a martyr, a witness of the divine word unless you are strengthened by the Holy Spirit. That is why the Savior says to the Apostles: and ye shall take power when the Holy Spirit descends. If you do not receive this power, you will not be able to be witnesses".

Saint Theophan the Recluse writes: "Grace, as the Saints tell us, makes us despise all". Not allowing ourselves to be imbued with the spirit of the world which assails us from all directions is a work of grace, an assistance, and gift from God. Grace gives us strength to resist the worldly spirit. We can resist the attraction of the world only with the grace of the Holy Spirit. That is why it is so important not to lose it. Only with it, are we able to resist this stream which seems to overflow everywhere: the spirit of worldly vanity. If we do not know how to preserve grace, we will have an empty, worldly, caricatured spiritual life, even if we are part of the worshiping Orthodox Church. We will have access to the grace of the Holy Spirit, but we will not be able to preserve it. And it will be even more difficult to preserve this grace as we get closer to the time of the end of the world. It is said that the evil one *must be released for a little while* (Revelation: 20:3)".

This is the spirit of secularization: you have the same grace, but you cannot use it because you do not know how, or you do not want to preserve it. Those who live like this are in the same situation as the foolish virgins. Although they are virgins, which means that they have done good deeds through which they receive grace, their lamps are empty – namely, they do not have the grace of the Holy Spirit.

The Worldly Spirit, Spirit of Vanity or the Antichrist Spirit

Saint Tikhon of Zadonsk says, "When vanity gets in the heart, eternity gets out." But what is vanity? In the *Egyptian Paterikon* it is said that "all that man thinks, below heaven, are vanities". And Saint John Chrysostom says: "All that do not pass along with us to heaven are worldly lusts, and all that remains in this world are worldly lusts. So, we have nothing in common with this".

Vanity is the same as the worldly spirit. **Therefore, vanity has the role of attracting people and making them deviate from God. The spirit of vanity blows like a wind on the broad path.** Vanity strives incessantly to attract the man to the broad path.

Saint Paisios of Mount Athos says: "Our thoughts are the most powerful foe of our soul's salvation, even more, powerful than the devil itself, is the **worldly spirit;** because it attracts us in a pleasant way, but in the end, it will embitter us forever". Regarding the importance of knowing this spirit, and how to keep ourselves away from it, Saint John of Kronstadt warns us: "by **not knowing the spirit that destroys, you will not know the Spirit that gives life.**"

How are we supposed to understand the difference? Saint Theophan the Recluse says: "Do not think that everything you do for your house and household is vanity. No, there are commandments for that, and the due fulfillment of such duties is among those things which please God. Do them all according to God's will, as is His command to you. Before anything call upon Him for help, then ask him for advice, and after completing it, thank God. By performing house duties, it will be as if you are fulfilling your prayer rule".

"Family problems are not vanities either; it is enough to take care of them with a good conscience and without breaking the divine law.

Vain acts are those which aim at satisfying passions and sins, as well as unnecessary and unhelpful things. Therefore separate vain worries from other concerns, which are not vain. The latter ones are always to God's will. Even more: they may occur to God's glory".

Saint Apostle Paul says: *But this I say, brethren, the time is short, so that from now on even those who have wives should be as though they had none, those who weep as though they did not weep, those who rejoice should be as though they did not rejoice, those who buy as they did not possess and those who use this world as not misusing it. For the form of this world is passing away* (Corinthians 7:29-31).

Saint Tikhon of Zadonsk says too: "He who loves God does not love the world."

Saint Nicodemus of the Holy Mountain writes: "Saint Basil the Great says: The ones who trample under feet worldly things and rise above them are witnessed as being worthy of the gift of the Holy Spirit (*On the Holy Spirit*). The reason why today we, both Christians and monks, are not worthy of the gifts of the grace of the Holy Spirit is that we have infatuation and love for the corruptible and transitory things of this world; and because **we also admire them and do not despise them as we should**. That's why a wise parent who sees his children admiring little, insignificant things such as toys, dice and other similiar things**, is not convinced to give them his wealth because he knows that if they do not know its value, they despise and lose it.** And he gives it to them when he sees that they have reached maturity and that they despise childish things. In the same way, God is not convinced to give us the wealth of His Grace, because He sees that we are just like ignorant children, admiring those things which are vain and which quickly vanish rather than loving spiritual and heavenly things, like mature men. If He gives it to us, we will despise it and lose it easily**,** and then we will be punished even more. Saint John Chrysostom also explains this in his eloquent and easy language: *He who admires the present things will never be worthy of the contemplation of the future things, but he who overlooks them and deems that they are nothing better than a shadow and a dream, will soon reach the spiritual ones. Because only then we show our children the wealth which befits men when we see that they have grown into men and overlooked all the childish things; but until they get to admire those things we deem them as unworthy of them.* (To Stelios, about piercing 2:2) ".

How the Holy Spirit is Ousted

The Holy Spirit is ousted first by the great sins, such as pride, wrath, having no mercy and damning our peers. The way in which the spirit of anger straitens and ousts grace is described in *The Shepherd of Hermas*: "But if any angry temper approach, forthwith the Holy Spirit, being delicate, is straitened, and not having the place clean, it seeks to retire from the place. For it is choked by the evil spirit, and does not have the liberty of serving the Lord as it would; for it is grieved by anger".

This happens not only with the spirit of anger but with any other spirit which is foreign to Christ, a cunning spirit, an unclean spirit or a deceptive spirit which someone receives in his soul. The Holy Spirit is ousted not only by great sins but also in other subtle ways through which a crafty and deceiving spirit pervades the soul. Saint Silouan the Athonite says: "He who reads bad books or journals **is hit by soul hunger**". "You should not be curious; you should not read worldly journals or books which **desolate the soul** and bring about ugliness and disquiet". We wonder what sin there is in flipping through newspapers. There is no such thing in the usual confession guides. But...this can oust grace. So, it is very, very important. It is because the newspapers create a whole atmosphere with an alien, cunning, and deceiving spirit, which straitens and finally ousts the grace of the Holy Spirit. It deflects attention to something else; by twisting meanings, intoxicating, anesthetizing and striking the Christian away from the narrow path.

The narrow path has the Holy Spirit, and the broad path has many, many cunning, deceiving, and vain spirits. Their name is "legion". This is the world of delusion, a world distant from the Holy Spirit, where man's soul is hungry and full of the spirit of vanity. **When the heart fills with the spirit of vanity, grace leaves us**. Or if it doesn't leave us right away, it is straitened, and we become close to losing it. We are certain that grace becomes straitened when we flip through newspapers and we suspect that it is straitened in many, many other daily life situations.

Saint Silouan the Athonite says: The Lord loves man so much, that He gives him the gifts of the Holy Spirit, but **until the soul learns to preserve grace, it struggles a lot**. Blessed is he who does not lose the grace of God, but rises from strength to strength".

Grace needs time to bear fruit in the human heart; it is just like a plant that is uprooted after sprouting. And again, seeds are planted in the earth, but uprooted again, and it never gets to bear fruit although we may have seeded the earth thousands of times. As Saint John Chrysostom says: "After baptism, over time, St. Paul became much brighter, and **grace was flowering even more in him**".

About Worldly People

Most businessmen, artists or even manual laborers, who speak with confidence and delight about their work, their mind, thoughts and skills, profit and quality and level of civilization, and many others, spread vain waves, which attract and conquer and subjugate hearts devoid of anything or filled to some extent with vanity. But, to those overshadowed by the Holy Spirit they look somehow stupid, rude, greedy, lovers of pleasures, saying and doing nothing to remind or be like the saints, completely ignoring the Gospel commandments. Be aware of what attracts you!

Saint Basil the Great says: "When someone boasts about his beauty or other traits or about the glamorous lives of his parents then his soul does not boast in the Lord; someone like this boasts about vanities. Those who practice different arts have nothing to boast of either: leaders, medical doctors, speakers or architects, who build fortresses or pyramids or mazes or other costly buildings or colossal constructions. **Those who boast with all these do not have their soul in the Lord**". Saint Silouan the Athonite says: He who has within himself the peace of the Holy Spirit, this peace will overflow to others, and he who has within himself the evil spirit, this evil will overflow on to others.

Just as the saints' hearts become *a river of living, life-giving water* (John 7:38), the people full of the spirit of vanity, their heart overflows with a river of cloudy, muddy, death-giving water.

It is obvious that the people filled with the spirit of vanity are exuding something around themselves, and they feed and water some people's souls and plant in their souls this "something".

In the sense mentioned above, any worker or intellectual who speaks with delight about his work or occupations, this means worldly things, pours forth from himself cloudy water and not life-giving water.

Any man who speaks with delight about his hobbies, his diplomas, his properties or even his skills, not to mention entertainment and luxury and wealth and pleasures, spreads around him death-giving, not life-giving, water.

At first, the noise of the overflowing water attracts, because just like the saints, these servants of vanity overflow something. But their water is cloudy and death bearing, and for those who have never seen another kind of water, it is even their very food and drink. And if one tries to stop them from drinking this, for them it seems like you want that they not to eat or drink anything at all. That is why they will hate you and will forsake you as an evil.

Saint John of Kronstadt about the Spirit of Vanity

"The Christian, who is called to a heavenly country, who is only a stranger and a pilgrim upon earth, ought not to attach his heart to anything earthly". "The Devil still lives and works in our hearts through our attachments to earthly things". "Attachment to the world is a delusion of the Devil, and is his spirit". "The material objects to which we attach ourselves in our hearts, which we passionately desire or grudge others, kill the soul by withdrawing it from God, the Source of life".

"Attachment to earthly things is idolatry". "When the heart is occupied with worldly things, especially superfluous ones, it forsakes the Lord". "Our attachments to earthly things will increase in proportion as our faith in heavenly blessings and love for them are getting weaker and weaker". "A momentary feeling of attachment to earthly things, or a momentary inclination of the heart to sin, a momentary doubt in the truth, and Satan penetrates into the heart, producing in a moment some violent passion in it, and afterwards, according to the measure of our sympathy with such a passion, he takes possession of us and drags us where he pleases as prisoners, bound hand and foot".

"We notice in ourselves the struggle between faith and unbelief, between the good power and the evil one; and in the world, **between the spirit of the Church and the spirit of the world**. There, through the spirit, you will distinguish two clearly antagonistic sides: the side of light and the side of darkness; of good and evil; the spirit of the Church and religion, and the spirit of worldliness and unbelief. Do you know why it is so? It is owing to the struggle between two antagonistic forces: of the power of God and the power of the Devil. The Lord works in the sons who are obedient to Him, and the Devil in the sons of disobedience (*the spirit that now works in the children of disobedience* Ephesians 2:2). And I, too, often feel within me the struggle of the same two antagonistic forces. When I stand up to pray, the evil force sometimes painfully oppresses and weighs down my heart, so that it cannot raise itself to God."

"Do not rejoice at gain, but let your only and constant joy be to win the Lord Himself. Trust entirely in Him: He knows how to lead you safely through this present life, and to bring you to Himself--into His eternal Kingdom.""Look upon everything in this world as upon a fleeting shadow, and do not cling with your heart to anything; do not consider anything in this world great, and do not lay your hopes upon anything earthly. Cling to the One imperishable, invisible, most wise God. We look not at the things which are seen, but at the things which are not seen; for the things which are seen are temporal, but the things which are not seen are eternal. (2 Cor 4:18)".

The Allure of the Spirit of Vanity

I have often wondered about the expression of satisfaction, wisdom, and peace which I usually notice on the face of someone smoking. And I think that they get in touch by this *sacrifice* with the spirit of vanity. As **the Holy Spirit mysteriously teaches people unspeakable mysteries, the unclean spirit mysteriously teaches them the mysteries of impiety and denying God**. They feel somehow more enriched from their contact with vanity than simple people. Not only the smokers but also the drunken, fornicators, pampered people, singers, yogis and followers of different falsehoods seem to have something more when compared to other people. Just like the people filled with the Holy Spirit are called spirits and serve God, we may call the others unclean spirits that work all kinds of evil. This is the state desired by those who are entirely bodies to animate themselves, motivate and have a goal.

That which is born of the Spirit is spirit"(John 3:6).

Saint John of Kronstadt says: "we either draw near to God, and become one spirit with Him, or withdraw ourselves from Him, and become one spirit with the Devil".

A meeting with powerful local men fills the soul with vain delight, in a special manner. The same happens sometimes just being around them, being able to see or enter their houses, their cars, their properties and companies and their vain and glamorous goods, appreciated, wanted and worshiped by the masses of the people who do not have the Holy Spirit in their hearts. The spirit of vanity works powerfully sometimes, even if it only means hearing the name of mammon's servants when seeing and hearing news about them in the newspapers and on the TV.

This vain delight is a sign that man is under the influence of the spirit of vanity. He may be delighted by his work or the work of others, his things or others things or by the athletic performance of his body or that of others. Often, he is amazed with a vain amazement, visiting churches and monasteries and talking to renowned confessors or even talking with Christians about God. And then they move on to other things which delight them. Of course, because they have good manners they may thank God for their good traits which are also 'delightful', but their hearts are drunk with vanities.

Everything that delights you makes your heart give an inappropriate importance to a thing, to get bound to that thing, to get bound to the earth (instead of becoming unbound and spiritually resurrected, you get bound and spiritually die). You get a thrill from counting money, when you receive money, when you make plans, when you imagine how much money you will earn, what business you will do, when you cheat, you get amazed by your skills, when you scoff and belittle others, when you laugh, when you go to the theater, or to shows, when you listen to music, you drink, you eat, you get into a restaurant, when you do something that few people can afford to do, when you travel, even when going to holy sites some people instead of piety feel delight that they arrived where others have not. You are in awe when you rise on the wings of dreaming, when you are close to the powerful people of the day, hearing about them, reading about them, and talking about them. You feel great happiness when talking about things you have done, about your memories, your friends, your school, your country and other people's country, your nation or other people's nation, you are amazed by electronics, games and computers, by telephones, clothes, cars, stores, football teams, singers, colors, lights, health, muscles, estate, by meeting with the spiritual fathers, you marvel with real or imaginary reasoning, or without any reason, or you laugh foolishly or you are amazed by your seriousness. All of them are one and the same thing, if you are amazed by them and its opposite, at the same time because it binds you to the earth, it banishes piety, and makes an abode in the heart to the worldly spirit.

Vain people love to see how others are also caught and filled with the spirit of vanity, how masses of people leap being fulfilled with the spirit of vanity which makes them look alive. But they are dead, puppets in the devils hands, filled with the spirit of vanity.

Worldly people cannot preserve the Grace

On the word that *many will seek to enter the Kingdom of God and will not be able* (Luke 13:24): what does that mean, many will seek to enter the Kingdom of God? It means that they will fast or will give alms or will refrain and will guard purity or will make abode in the wilderness, or will not eat meat or drink wine or will give money to the poor or to the Church or will confess and receive The Holy Eucharist or all of the above and still will not enter the Kingdom of God. And others will be monks, and others priests and others will pray a lot and will read akathists and will endeavor according to the word *those who strive to enter the Kingdom of God*, but despite all their endeavor, they will not be able to enter.

But…they did good deeds. Yes, but so did the foolish virgins as St. Seraphim of Sarov explains concerning the foolish virgins that they had done good deeds, but they did not have the grace of the Holy Spirit. And, in *The Shepherd* it is said that the Holy Spirit and the spirit of anger (and probably the spirit of vanity) cannot dwell in the human soul at the same time. So, man can do good deeds, but if the spirit of vanity dominates in his heart, he will not enter the Kingdom of God, because we cannot serve two masters at the same time.

"The spirit of vanity fills the empty ones" (it says in *The Shepherd*) which means those without the grace of the Holy Spirit. So, the empty ones fill, are filled and will be filled with the worldly spirit. From where? From parties, festivals, and theaters. And nowadays: in supermarkets, pubs, nightclubs, shows, concerts, sport matches or with the TV and the internet. The worldly books or even the books in the school book lists. Those who connect to these works are filled with the spirit of vanity (most of the times) and drive out the Holy Spirit from their souls. Besides, the Church says that if someone dies in a state of being drunk, he will not achieve salvation. But, what would happen with those who would die in pubs, by drugs or when watching television? Sins drive out the Holy Spirit, but this is not the issue here. It is about those apparently harmless things which deprive us of God and of the Kingdom of God. Those whom the devil does not trap by fornication or anger or pride, he will fill them with vanities so that the likeness to God will be erased from their soul.

Actually, how many "well-intentioned men" do you know, who are connected to the spirit of vanity, participate in these vain "events" and thus committing in their hearts the liturgy of vanity.

…*The Spirit of truth, whom the world cannot receive*, John (14:17).

Some will do good deeds, they will even go to Church, but if vanity dwells in their hearts everything will be distorted and wrong.

When the Holy Spirit dwells in man's heart, Saint Symeon the New Theologian says, it mysteriously advises the person in all places about what to do, and how to do it. It also says that where the spirit of vanity dwells, impudence, and love of indecency enters instead of the virtue of Christian humility. And again, these people may also do good deeds, and some of them will strive a lot spiritually, but even in their current state, although they may do great things if they cannot separate from the spirit of vanity, it is still not enough. *"If anyone does not have the Spirit of Christ, he is not His"* (Romans 8:9)". *"For as many as are lead by the Spirit of God, these are sons of God.* (Romans 8:14)".

The work of the foolish virgins

He who is filled with vanities is like a man who must go on a journey. He packs his luggage and dresses, but when he is about to leave, he sees himself suddenly undressed and with his luggage scattered, and then he puts them in order but afterwards they are scattered again. He is not nailed in the chains of the deadly sins, but despite this, he is not able to leave. Does it not seem that the unwise virgins were rightly called foolish? Is this not a state of madness?

But the spirit of vanity is the one which is working. Yes, let's visit some friends and when we are there let's talk about many worldly things, listen to news, thumb through the newspapers, talk about the football match, or even read a book of poems where the poet has some amazing verses.

Yes, I haven't slandered, I haven't judged, I have had no thoughts of fornication, but I am still, overall, full of the spirit of vanities. The grace of God could not enter our hearts or if it did during prayer or during the Church services, it was immediately driven out and replaced with worldly concerns which filled our hearts, so that today we were finally defeated, even if we thought we were full of good deeds.

"I was at church, but now I'm watching a movie". This is the work of the foolish virgins. After they strain to bring grace into their hearts, then they surround it with vanities, so that finally it is forced to get out (or rather, they drive it out by pushing a button).

And there will come a time when the Lord will say to them: Why didn't you come to Me, when I was close, and nothing hindered you? You were ready to start the journey but you couldn't. Others, bound with heavy chains, stripped them off the walls and came to Me with chains and all, and you couldn't because you preferred to watch TV serials (and to listen to vanities)? Others had heavy sins and yet, they came, and you, even though you did good deeds, could not come? Isn't this madness? Why did you even do them, if you haven't picked up the fruits, if you haven't let grace fill your heart? You are like a man who prepares to have lunch but because he has dirty hands, he washes them. But again the dirt of worldliness soils them , and he washes his hands again. And this goes on and on, and he is not able to taste much of the good food in front of him.

God will judge you according to what he will find in your heart.

Never has it been easier to obtain the salvation of your soul than now. Now, not watching TV and not reading and seeing and listening to vanities looks like the most extreme fast, not fornicating looks like striving as a hermit on a pillar, and having a beard or being unadorned and not wearing make-up, dressing decently and going to church looks like confessing Christ in front of pagans and idols worshipers.

Grace helps the ones who are striving

The things which are impossible with men are possible with God (Luke 18:27). Man is often very helpless. He cannot fast, he cannot pray, he cannot leave vanities, he cannot live without TV, without matches, without movies, without vain discussions, without new clothes, luxury and comfort.

And yet, there is a mysterious way to overcome this! When man soars to surpass one of these barriers, to do something which seems to him impossible, to get a little closer to God, then the Holy Spirit comes to help him. It comes to aid our weakness. Notice how we are able to attract the Holy Spirit to our heart, trying to do these things which are otherwise impossible, especially now at the end times. Someone attracts the Holy Spirit to his rescue starting to fast, someone else by prayers. And, the Holy Spirit will come and will help them so that the servant of God will not be ashamed. Another one, although he has no money, desires to give alms to someone who has less than him. And then the Holy Spirit will come to his help either by giving him what he needs through different means or will comfort his heart with such an abundance of sweetness, that it will be greater than any material good.

That is why repentance is so important. The sinner says from the bottom of his heart "I'll never do that again". And others comment: "it is impossible for him to leave sin aside". But, when the Holy Spirit sees a genuine desire on the part of the sinner to straighten himself out, it comes quickly to enhance that intention which pleases God. It comes with its grace to touch, sweeten, advise and resurrect the dead soul, who is repentant. Repentance is not a sad moment after which the Christian will be scrutinized by God, but it is the very way in which the sinful soul attracts to it the grace of the Holy Spirit which comes to work together with the repenting soul, the lost sheep deeply loved. It is impossible to draw yourself from worldly vanities on your own. But, if you want this with a genuine heart, the Holy Spirit will come to your aid with full power, and will dwell in your heart to carry out this work that pleases God.

Similarities

There is a certain light on the faces of those who are filled with the spirit of vanity. On the outside, they take an angelic face, but the Evil One dwells in their hearts. We can see everywhere rich men, politicians, movie stars, singers or people living in debauchery who seem to shed a certain light, yet all of this is nothing but delusion. Saint John of Kronstadt says: "Do not rejoice when your countenance is bright from pleasant food and drink, because then the inward face of your soul is hideous and deadly, and at that time the words of the Savior Christ are applicable to you: *For you are like unto whited sepulchers, which, indeed, appear beautiful outward, but are within full of dead men's bones* (Matthew 23:27) that is, of hypocrisy and iniquity."

There are certain similarities between those possessed by the spirit of vanity and saints: they both look alive, they are both powerfully ruled by something. But believers often seem reluctant in their actions, sometimes moved a little by the Holy Spirit, and other times pushed into action by the spirit of vanity. Instead, the vessels of vanity act with confidence, power and force, and in the eyes of those who are not spiritual they seem amazing, powerful, full of strength and worthy of esteem, but, for to the spiritual ones they are puppets in the hands of the devils, scornful men and Satan's apostles.

Also, the vain vessels and the Saints are a little fought by the devils, the latter because they burn the demons, and the former due to the logistics of the demons' attacks against mankind. They are already conquered; the attacks should be directed somewhere else. What happens with the sinner who commits sins? Isn't he actually under the guidance of the spirit of vanity? Isn't he inclined to laugh, or to ironies and does not he seek to fill his soul with vain joy? No one can enter the Kingdom without the Holy Spirit, as Saint Symeon the New Theologian says, even if he commits no sins (but, this is impossible), they would be the inheritors of hell.

So, the devils and the angels fight especially for those in the middle, for those who have a few good deeds, who are sons of the Church, but who are attracted to the spirit of vanity and, therefore, cannot become vessels of the Holy Spirit.

It is the same in Church, there are similarities between the servants of God and those who receive the word with joy by participating in religious services but have no roots, do not know how to preserve the grace and lose it and squander it easily. They both meet in church, they greet each other and seem to be one and the same, alike. But some preserve and multiply the grace and others squander it when they get out of church.

Ultimately, man is animated by the Holy Spirit or by the spirit of vanity. Yet there is a middle state when it moves by the natural laws or its natural traits, when it is not filled with anything. But we believe that this happens only seldom, and it is rather a temporary state when the ruling spirit decreases for a while. Because afterward, some are thirsty for parties, booze, idle talk and anything else that will fill them with the spirit of vanity again. And others thirst to attend church and to read spiritual books and prayer books. Some feel full of the ruling spirit in clubs, at sport matches or shows or shopping in the supermarket, while others feel full in church and when praying. People look alike in this state when the ruling spirit is decreasing. But then, some soar towards life and other towards vanity. Some go on towards good health, others towards sickness. And they try to get filled with that spirit mastering them and then they feel they are swallowed by the spirit of vanity – some of them, and others – by the Holy Spirit.

Yet if the Holy Spirit is absent, man will not be able to properly comprehend the writings of the Holy Fathers, the Bible. He will not comprehend the purpose of the Sacraments and the importance of the Church. He will see that he and the Protestants, the yogis, and others have the same master spirit. And he will come to the conclusion that there is no difference between the Church and other spiritual practices. Although he has heard that it is not good to pray together with heretics, oriental practices or others, his heart will still feel a kinship, likeness, and attraction to them. And however proficient in theology he might be, if he does not become a vessel of the Holy Spirit, he will feel irresistibly attracted to the spirit of vanity. Just like the Spiritual people say "it is not me who is living, but Christ is living within me," those full of the spirit of vanity are the ones through whom the devil speaks, works, sings, and dances. And the devils may be theologians and the vessels of vanity may sometimes be theologians, even very good ones. And they will inevitably be attracted to ecumenism, to technology and profane culture, and to other organizations outside the Church.

The Fulfilled Man

I have often heard the expression "fulfilled man" and people indicated a man in possession of a house, a car, a beautiful wife, a business. At first, I thought that since Christ is not within that man, he could not be a truly fulfilled man. Then, I understood that there was more to it. This man is not only far from Christ, like even the believers are often, but he is also a man full of the spirit of vanity.

Saint Lawrence of Chernigov says this about the Antichrist: "it will be very nice for the sinners, but the devout will see it as frightening". And Saint John of Kronstadt says that: "it will have eyes like embers, a fierce face, and it will be cunning, insidious and frightful". And all its servants will be the same. They will look handsome and radiant, but for the believers, they will be frightful.

A fulfilled man in the eyes of this world means a man filled with the spirit of vanity. Since sometimes the world tells the truth, albeit unwittingly, or without comprehension. Indeed such a man can be considered fulfilled, but not filled with what he should be filled with, but with what he should not be. He is filled not with the heavenly ones but with the earthly ones.

Christ referred to such men when He said: *Get behind Me, Satan! You are an offense to Me, for you are not mindful of the things of God, but the things of men* (Matthew 16:23). And they are an offense to us every day, when we see them parading on the TV screens or exposing their devilish brilliance through different occasions. But, for believers, they were, are and will be frightening.

It is a very high aspiration to intend to get filled with the Holy Spirit. And when talking about it, it seems that we are talking about something which is hard to attain. But, when we are talking about the spirit of vanity, it is not like this at all. We all know it, we feel it, we are full of it, we often want it, and we almost cannot live without it. We all know the pleasure of going shopping, of watching TV, of seeing funny shows, matches and sport competitions, of indulging our minds with dreams and imaginations, of admiring our appearance, our clothes or our cars, of reading poetry or novels, and of navigating the internet. It is the spirit of vanity which fills the ones without the grace of the Holy Spirit.

You feel the spirit of vanity when it comes, you feel how it fills you. You feel it when you sweeten up beyond measure with vain things, whatever they might be. Are we not talking about sins and about something else which is well known (due to the bad fruits). Do we really exaggerate?! If we really want to receive and get filled with the Holy Spirit, we do not exaggerate. Saint John Chrysostom says that God: "Calling mankind to heaven and to the heavenly rewards claimed, on the other hand, the contempt of the goodies from earth".

The young man in the Gospel was also doing good deeds, but he was not on the way; because he was possessed by the spirit of vanity. Christ told him : "*sell all that you have*" (Luke 18:22) but, He could tell others: don't watch matches anymore, if you want to attain holiness, or give up TV or vain parties or don't go to the beach in the summer, if you want to be a true Christian.

Wherever you turn, especially in these times, you see, you taste, or you get filled with vanities. Or you are fighting not to have your soul filled with them.

And the Holy Spirit also said that these people full of the spirit of vanity say: "*I am rich, have become wealthy, and have need of nothing – and do not know that you are wretched, miserable, poor, blind and naked* (Revelation 3:16)".

We are not referring here to those who are far from the Church, but to those who come to Church, even on a regular basis, but they also forsake regularly Christ, and they fill with the spirit of vanity. They are lukewarm Christians who cannot see their sins, who don't fight against them, who are praised and brag like the pharisee with his illusive justice. How many of us are just the same?! We all are, perhaps, more or less. In different times and places, today and yesterday, and last year. And first of all I, who am writing these lines, I have been filled with vanities. Even today. And yesterday.

That is why we speak about the Holy Spirit, as about something that vanished from the earth. Because we chose to get filled with "something else". And to serve someone else. But, with the help of God, the lover of mankind, we hope and believe that we can find the way.

Contemporary view

Trilling picture: Millions of people receiving grace in Church and then wasting it in a few hours or minutes. In one or two hours they immerse themselves again into the ocean of vanities and grace drifts away. People say incredulously: "I don't feel anything; it is useless to me; there is no grace in Church". There is grace, but we don't know how to keep it. Why do you run after grace in far-away places, if you waste it later, so easily afterward?

It is of utmost importance not to waste, scoff or scorn grace after we have received it. No matter how much grace the soul receives it will not benefit the soul, if it cannot preserve it. Wasting the received grace has become a widespread habit. Perplexed by their inability to preserve grace, some Christians choose to join the neo-Christian cults. There is no grace there, only the spirit of vanity, which fills up their souls. The spirit of vanity is not driven away by sins, but rather it is fed and enhanced by them. The unclean (vain) seed grows and starts sprouting in their hearts. Any sins they would do, this spirit remains inside them. You will even hear these unhappy people say: "this is something different, now I am really making progress". But, the progress is into Satan. It is impossible to both live in callousness and vanities and to be full of the grace of the Holy Spirit. But to be full of the spirit of vanity is possible. It is Satan's solution for our modern times. The good done by these people cannot be received in heaven. It doesn't build anything for them there. But God, in order not to remain in debt, rewards them here, on earth. Their worldly progress is considered a proof of divine protection when it actually is a sign of forsakenness. They will receive everything here, and nothing will remain for them there. If your good is not received in heaven, you will receive everything here, on earth. And if it is received up there, you will receive indescribable reward.

Just as Christians who listen to religious songs receive the grace of the Holy Spirit to some extent, in the same way, Christians who listen to worldly music fill themselves with the worldly spirit; the devilish spirit; the spirit of vanity, In the same way the Christians look at icons and listen to the word of God and they are filled with grace, worldly people look at newspapers, magazines, listen to the radio and TV and fill with the spirit of vanity. Just as the Christian enters the House of God and is filled with grace, the same Christian may become filled with the worldly spirit when entering stores, banks, pubs, educational institutions or other buildings, centers of the vain worldly power. He feels an inexplicable delight and fulfillment, and he will be thirsty again for it. Just like a Christian fills with joy and grace attending the Church services and meeting with the representatives of God and seeing and listening to them, the same Christian may fill up with the worldly spirit (and with vain amazement) attending concerts, theaters, sport matches and shows and when they meet actors, sportsmen, celebrities, and all the other representatives through whom the devil's deception works.

Those who worship the material world worship the Antichrist who tries to make them forgot the Kingdom of Heaven and what man was meant to be. Those who worship science, culture, art, and other worldly skills also worship the Antichrist. Because by worshiping them, they worship either the material goods produced by them or the comfort provided by them; or they worship the worldly and awe-inspiring vanity produced by them. Those who boast and seek to exalt in all that, seek to exalt in material goods over divine goods. They show that they do not know and do not have any spiritual experience, and therefore they speak only about what they know. They believe that the scientist and the hermit do the same work, when they actually do two different works, as the first is oriented to the corruptible earth and the hermit to the Heavenly Kingdom.

You cannot separate worshiping science and worshiping material goods or worshiping worldly culture and the spirit of vanity.

Saint John of Kronstadt writes: "God drove apart from human hearts and does not reign in them, because there the cunning spirit reigns full of deception and alienation from God; man turned himself into the devil's workshop, **a laboratory of the evil devils**, which build in it all the deception, all the evil".

What I feel when I get filled up with the worldly spirit

An amazement which is rather a hectic state, the desire to speak, to laugh, to make jokes, to brag, to admire the rich and those enhanced by vanities who seem handsome, powerful and who attract irresistibly (as Saint Lawrence says that Antichrist will be).

Some isolate themselves from people and speak with the devils which imagine and paint vanities in their mind. They feel the need to read about the great vain people of the world, to read in the newspapers about them, to see photos, news, and films with them.

But, what can I do then? Should I not do anything at all? It is one thing to take have many concerns, and another to get filled with vanity. The first drives us away from God, and the second is to cleave to Satan, to look and share in his things.

But, having many cares causes us to lose our concern for God and empties the soul. It prepares the land for the spirit of vanity, which is not else than to dance to the rhythm of the devil, to bathe in its spirit and to be deluded, as Saint Ignatius explains very well: "to consider the truth as a lie and the lie as a truth". Those who care for a lot of things and empty themselves from God feel that they make an effort to pray and go to Church, but to bathe in vanities needs no effort at all.

Forgetfulness of God and attachment to Satan are two things which lead in the same direction. The direction to hell, on the wide way that seems easier. But to forget about God and then to remember Him are two opposite works. Doing both is somehow senseless, a fact also noticed by the unbelievers. In reply, they choose to advance decidedly, but toward hell, under the guidance of Satan. I don't like this determination of the unbelievers; I prefer the Christians' indecisiveness (fight). We cannot forsake any sin without God's help, nor can we forsake the love for vanities.

What shall I do then? If I get filled with vanities when I have money, what shall I do? If when my business is successful, I get filled up with vanities, what shall I do, shall I give them up? I'm not saying you must always give everything up. But if you do that at least once, you will get filled with great power. What if you have a lot of money, and you rejoice in vain? Give a part to the poor or the Church. Give until the vain joy disappears. But what if I am rejoicing foolishly even for a small coin, even if I cannot buy anything with it? You are in a vile state, oh man! Give even this one too, and you'll feel released. Think of Abraham, who had a lot of riches but he was upright in heart, and not vain, but you celebrate and jump over a trifle? You must really give all that you have so that you might follow God. But, Abraham (or Job) the blessed did not have to forsake all his possessions for he owned them as if he did not have them.

This vile state is not for any other cause, except because the seed of the Holy Spirit planted in baptism has not grown in our hearts. To not fill easily with vanities is a sign of spiritual growth and a sign that you are not on the wide way. It is the refusal to worship the idols of our times.

But vain amazement is followed by disappointment. Older people are not so much attracted by vanities because they have the memory of so many disappointments. It is really sad to see old people full of the spirit of vanity, and it is a great honor and joy when young people strive to get out of it. God comes to their rescue most of the times.

When we see a soul filling up with vanities, for one thing, we see that we distance it from God's care, so that soul does not to get injured by it. Sometimes what we pray for is given to us, but it is then taken away from us because it is harmful. Someone may not find a job, if it injures him, it makes him chat, laugh, tell jokes, forget about eternal life and be filled with vanities. In a more modest position, it will be easier for him to be humble, exhausting all worldly solutions, he will also reach God; he will also have more time to read and go to Church. When most people find worldly wealth, they say: *Soul, you have many goods laid up for many years; take your ease; eat, drink and be merry* (Luke 12, 19). They have become filled. but this type of fulfilled man is full of the spirit of vanity.

The prophets are called whistles through which the Holy Spirit is blowing, but there are also whistles of the spirit of Antichrist: singers, movie stars, celebrities, worldly people who are seen and admired by masses of people. They also sing something and attract people with their songs, but the singer is the devil and those who listen to him either go closer to the cunning singer, losing the right way, or they stop in a certain place and do not move forward more on the way (where the other song can be heard: the song of the Holy Spirit). Travelers gather around the cunning singer, who tells them that they must not go anywhere, but stay there in that bazaar and get sweetened with candies and swing in dizzying swings. Meanwhile, the accomplices of the cunning singer rob the travelers' luggage in search for pure gold, purified seven times, very valuable, gathered by them through ascetic effort, patience, and Church Sacraments. The travelers will tear up bitterly seeing that they were robbed; they will become desperate and only seldom they will go away from there, from that cunning bazaar, with cunning rules and attractive ways, but which drag us away more and more from The Path to Salvation.

Abroad

What happens to people who go abroad?

The people who partake of the spirit of vanity and find their happiness in the spirit of vanity, to a greater or lesser extent are amazed, awestruck, hypnotized, delighted and subjugated by the overflow of the spirit of vanity which is there. This even happens to people who are filled only to a very small extent with the spirit of vanity, who seem pious, fair Christians and good parents. They will be changed and transformed by the overflow of vanity. Anyone who doesn't have in his soul the power of the grace of the Holy Spirit will not be able to oppose the attraction of the spirit of vanity. His soul will be invaded, subjugated by the devastating work of the devilish spirit of vanity. Both the Holy Spirit and the spirit of vanity work on the human soul and transform man.

In Society

If a man's heart is not full of the spirit of vanity, he cannot convincingly play any of the roles of the world's great stage. As Saint Symeon the New Theologian says: *Because a good man out of the good treasure of his heart brings forth good things, and an evil man out of the evil treasure brings forth evil things* (Matthew 12:35). And you see now the depths of the Spirit, as the Lord said not only that the good things come out of a good heart, but he also added that out of the treasure of his heart, to find out that **none of us can have an empty and light heart**, but everyone will have either the grace of the Spirit, through goodness and true faith, or they bear in themselves the wicked devil, because of lack of faith and carelessness toward the commandments and by being fulfilled with evil things".

About guarding against the spirit of vanity

Even if we know how the spirit of the world acts and manifests itself, if we read or even write a book about it, nevertheless if the Holy Spirit is not in my heart, I will not be able to oppose vanities and will be sweetened by, think of and frolic with delight in the multitude of material goods.

Those who watch sport matches take pride and exalt with the winners, those who watch TV serials take pride and delight in the characters who succeed. In this way they attach their mind to the wings of dreaming about vain people. Even in times of respite when they have no worries, instead of getting closer to God, they are concerned about the worries of characters in films. Those who watch shows partake in the vain glory of these, and in their minds they raise themselves on the wings of music and brilliant scenery.

You should no longer walk as the rest of the Gentiles walk, in the futility of their mind (Ephesians 4:17).

Just like those who are workers of the Jesus prayer for their heavenly Father, this prayer becomes self-working in the heart, so too with people under the influence of devilish illusions these become self-working in man's mind. Someone who saw several films, shows, 3-D games and accepted them recklessly, doesn't need anything more. The memory of these things appear and get out and are resurrected and recombine by themselves, helping the devilish spirit. One who listens for a period of time to music from Satan's concert, afterwards it seems that this is produced by itself in the mind.

This is a kind of temporary sealing engraved on his heart. But the man can be released if he turns back to Christ, back to Church and to holy things.

Getting Accustomed with the Vanity

There are certain similarities between the drunkenness caused by the spirit of vanity and that caused by alcoholic drinks. Likewise, there are some who resist becoming intoxicated and keep a certain lucidity, and others who get drunk and lose control as soon as they taste a little of the spirit of vanity, but they both intend to attain the state of drunkenness; and those who have a higher tolerance need to drink more, to drink from more vanities. And those who, at the beginning, used to get drunk immediately with the spirit of vanity, after a while develop such a high tolerance to those beverages that in order to get drunk they need either larger quantities or stronger beverages. Those strong beverages that seemed useless at first and somehow an embodiment of immoderation, have now become a necessity; because with the soft beverages of the beginning, the drinker of vanities doesn't feel anything anymore. He feels the deadly need for strong drinks and looks with spite at the beer drinkers or the drinkers of other soft beverages.

After a while of vanity consumption, like with alcoholics or drug-addicts the state of addiction is installed, people can no longer conceive life without their drug: without TV, without music, without stores, without football, without a car. And just like the alcoholics, they need a time of rehab, which seems to them extremely difficult, and they need a lot of care, but on one condition: a sincere desire to fight the passion (vanity). Also to such people are addressed the following words: "Keep your mind in hell and despair not".

Those who are not accustomed to drinking, for example children, get drunk with a small amount of vanities. He who is not accustomed to the vanities of the world can also get drunk with just the smallest amount.

If a spiritual man joins some men drunk with the drunkenness of vanities, it is just as if a nondrinker enters a pub. He will be lured with a glass, with different vanities, then he will be scoffed, slandered and finally drove out, if possible.

The drunkards boast to each other with how much they drank, what wines they tasted and, also the lovers of vanities share their impressions during the different parades vanity.

Longing for vanities

The human soul hates being empty. That is why man is advised to fill himself with the Holy Spirit, to go all the way with fulfilling the commandments, not omitting or ignoring anything. Because if he stops in the middle of the road, he will not get filled with the Holy Spirit and the human being cannot endure the emptiness. He will foolishly insist on getting filled with something, and he will get filled up with the spirit of vanity. (This is acedia: the longing for vanities)

Emptiness is hell for man. To endure the emptiness while waiting for grace is a hard struggle. "Keep your mind in hell, and despair not" says Saint Silouan the Athonite. Spiritual life oscillates between states of light filled grace and emptiness.

To endure the emptiness refusing to fill oneself up with the spirit of vanity is martyrdom. It is the martyrdom of Christians today.

However, the temptation is in accordance with each one's strength and also the state of emptiness is according to how much each can endure.

Saint John of Kronstadt says about amusements: "What does to seek amusement mean? It means to wish to fill somehow the sickly emptiness of the soul, which was created for activity, and which cannot bear to be idle". "What do theaters bring into the hearts of men? The spirit of this world, the spirit of idleness, of idle speaking, of joking, of cunning, and wickedness, of pride, presumption--they do not bring any moral good to anyone. The authors of the pieces and the actors only give people what they have in themselves, their own spirit, neither more nor less".

The spirit of vanity seeks to imitate the Holy Spirit

The spirit of vanity seeks to imitate the gifts of the Holy Spirit; there is a peace, a joy, and even a long patience. But how different they are: some rejoice to have untied the links with the world and get closer to Christ, and others rejoice to be immersed in the world and forgot about Christ. Some obtain peace by fasting and prayer, others by gluttony and frivolous entertainment. Some in loneliness, others in the middle of apostate masses. Some in the Church, others outside it.

Worldly people have their own peace, but if they don't have it through Christ it is a deceitful one, and they are thieves and robbers, and they will hear the words: *I am the door. He who does not enter by the door, but climbs up some other way, is a thief and a robber* (John 10:1-8).

The yogis also have their own peace, the rich men have a peace and a joy of their own, the culture lovers have something also. Men at the pubs also have a joy, but if it is without Christ (and how else could it be?), then it is deceitful. The joy can be only in the Holy Spirit, otherwise it is a lie.

And you He made alive, who were dead in trespasses and sins, in which you once walked according to the course of this world, according to the prince of the power of the air, the spirit who now works in the sons of disobedience, among whom also we all once conducted ourselves in the lusts of our flesh, fulfilling the desires of the flesh and of the mind, and were by nature children of wrath, just as the others (Ephesians 2:1-3).

News and Information

News definitely has a place these days in filling up the soul with vanities. The news we read or see on the internet or on television, whether it is about sports, fashion, politics, gastronomy, lifestyle, travel, products, elections or celebrities, and the advertisements that come with them, all fill us up with vanities. The Apostle Paul was greatly distressed when he saw that Athens was given over to idols and that all the Athenians and foreigners who lived there spent their time *in nothing else but either to tell or to hear some new thing.* (Acts 17:21).

Saint Nicodemus of the Holy Mountain says in *Unseen Warfare*: "The information, breaking news and all the transformations small or big and changes in the world and in your country should be for you as if nothing had happened. But, even if others bring them to you reject them, drive them away from your heart and imagination".

Besides the spiritual matters, he says further: "Any other issue, any other information, and curiosity is selfishness and pride. By these tools, the devil seeks to win the will of those who pay attention to spiritual life. It fights with all its powers and strives to defeat their minds with these kind of curiosities. By these means, he wants to conquer both mind and will. Therefore, it often seeks to give people even high, subtle and curious notions, especially to those who like to think about them and to those who quickly attach to them. Guided by passions, through discussion on these high notions by which they mistakenly deem to please God, they forget to clean their hearts".

"The ruler of this world is coming, and he has nothing in Me" (John 14:30). Who else can say that?

Saint Symeon the New Theologian says: **"The sign and the proof that the Kingdom of Heaven is inside us is the fact that we do not wish for anything from seen and**

corruptable things, meaning the things and delights of this world, neither wealth, nor glory, nor pleasure, nor any other delight of life and body, but to refrain ourselves and have a disposition of loathing from all these, as those dressed in clean clothes avoid the stench and mud". (So when all these advertisements we are surrounded by ignite in us the appetite and desire to have those things, the Kingdom of Heaven is no longer inside us. Is this not the work of Satan, with all these advertisements which assault us daily?)

Saint Symeon also says: "When you want to start eating, remember your sins and ask yourself: could it be my doom If I will eat any of the food in front of me?". We should ask ourselves the same question whenever we taste willingly, needfully or unwillingly, the sweet fruit of culture, science, and technology.

Final Advice

Saint John Chrysostom referring to the three young men from the fiery furnace says: "even now it is the King of Babylon, even now a flame bigger than that one is lit, even now there is a command to admire such an idol image. Even now satraps stand nearby, and soldiers and delightful music and many admire this mottled and big idol. ... But just as all these existed in the past, there are also today zealots like the three young men, who say: *We do not serve your gods nor will we worship the gold image which you have set up* (Daniel. 3:18), but we suffer the furnace of poverty and any uneasiness for the laws of God. And those who have much, like those from then, most of the times worship this image and burn for his love, while those who have nothing despise this image".

Saint Nikita Stithatos writes: "None of those who were baptized and believe in Christ remains deprived of the Spirit's grace unless they surrendered themselves to the whole work of the adverse spirit. But he who kept the fire of the Holy Spirit received at Holy Baptism untouched, or if it extinguished he invigorated it by good deeds, it is impossible not to receive gracefulness from above. And if someone is not an accomplice to any of these, **I cannot say that someone like this is a believer** or that he is numbered among those who have put on Christ from Holy Baptism".

Chapter 2

Blessed are the Poor in Spirit

The First Beatitude

In his commentary on the Beatitudes, Saint Gregory of Nyssa says: "The ones who climb a stair, climb the first step, and then they are lifted to the next step above it, and then again from the second step of the stair they are lifted to the third, and so on... **It seems to me that the string of the Beatitudes has the appearance of steps**; it explains how climbing is eased by passing from one step to another. Because if a person understands the First Beatitude, he will become prepared to understand the next and so on....even if these words seem to surprise at first sight".

What could be the meaning of the First Beatitude, and why do some Christians hurry to overlook it as something shameful? When actually, it is the foundation of spiritual growth and if we overlook the first step of the stair we will surely climb another stair, not the one that draws us to salvation.

Saint Symeon the New Theologian says: "Blessed are the poor in spirit means those who have not any thought of this century".

Blessed are the poor in spirit with a small "*s*". So, it is not about the Holy Spirit, but about any other foreign spirit, in particular, the worldly spirit, the spirit of vanity. Blessed are the poor in spirit are those who do not have the spirit of vanity filling their hearts? The Holy Apostle Paul specifies: "*We have received, not the spirit of the world, but the Spirit who is from God*" (1 Corinthians 2:12).

Saint Tikhon of Zadonsk explains what is the beginning of spiritual growth: "When we want our heart to be lightened with true knowledge of God, we must get the world out of our heart. Because the world is nothing but *the lust of the flesh, the lust of the eyes and pride of life* (1 John 2:16) which are all in the soul. All these should be banished from our soul so that the soul can be enlightened by true knowledge of God. The world and this enlightenment are things that do not fit each other: one must go out so that the second can come in. As much as the world gets out from our heart, so much so will the heart be enlightened".

"Bear well in mind that when, according to the word of God, you don't look for ephemeral wealth, honor, glory, pleasure, but you look for and want only the eternal treasure, then it will be opened for you in heaven, according to His promise, and the passion and the desire for ephemeral things will depart from you: so seek for the eternal goodness and do not desire ephemeral ones". "You can see, from all of the above which has been mentioned, that we are born and renewed with Holy Baptism, not for this world; otherwise we should remain in it forever, but we are born and renewed for passing into the next life. Those who seek here for honors, wealth and glory are sinners and prodigal sons. By endeavoring for these things, they reveal that their home is this world and that they want to live in it forever. They are like the traveler who, resting for a short while in a foreign country, builds an estate: houses, gardens, lakes and other such things, but when he returns home will have to leave them behind and return without any of them. Thus, we also enter this world for a short while, just like in a foreign country and, when we are getting out of it, we go to our own place: worshipers of God into eternal life and the non worshipers into eternal torments".

"When the Christian turns to the world and worldly things, he turns his back on God and heaven, and when he loves earthly things he moves his love away from the Creator, hence his heart moves away from God, attaching himself to created things, just like Adam stretched his hand to the forbidden tree. So, **this world is for us what the forbidden tree was for**

Adam, it is put here for our temptation. Now, to whom shall we turn our heart? To God or to the world? When we turn our heart to God, we will turn it away from the world. And when we turn it to the world, we will turn it away from God. It is not possible to love the world and God, as it is written: *If anyone loves the world, the love of the Father is not in him* (1 John 2:15). Just like God told Adam not to eat from that tree, He tells us now: do not love the world or worldly things. So, you can see why we should despise the world: to worship our God".

Saint John of Kronstadt says: "It is impossible to serve God truly and at the same time to be attached to earthly things, for all such things relate to mammon. All earthly things, if our heart attaches itself to them, make it gross and earthly, turn us away from God, from the Mother of God, and all the saints, from everything spiritual, heavenly, and eternal, and from love for our neighbor, and bind us to that which is earthly, perishable, and temporal. The spirit of attachment to earthly things, of sparing and grudging earthly things, is the spirit of the Devil, and the Devil himself dwells in the man through his attachment to earthly things."

Poorness in spirit and humility

Saint Symeon the New Theologian and Saint Ignatius Brianchaninov say: **Blessed are the poor in spirit, meaning those who have no thought for these times**.

But this is not all. "**Blessed are the poor in spirit means those who are humble**", explains Saint John Chrysostom. Here we are, in front of an apparent contradiction. We said before that the poor in spirit means those who are not full of vanities, poor in vanities. Actually, there is no contradiction in this, but rather a very important idea. Are those who are full of the spirit of vanity humble? He who gets filled up with vanities when he participates in a carnival or a concert or is successful in business and is in the world stream, is he humble? He who buys new, nice clothes and is delighted by them? He who boasts on various occasions? He who watches TV, is he humble? No, he raises his soul on the wings of vanity according to Satan's model and fills up with vain delight. People often take pride when their favorite football player won (in their minds, they are the ones full of glory, as the psychologists say). Since a man cannot be haughty with what he is and what he does, as much as he would like to boast, he seeks to raise himself through vanities. Namely to imagine that he is that actor or that singer (as the psychologists say, there is a dual personality known as schizophrenia). And he rejoices in that outpouring of acclaim as if it were fresh water from which he drinks and becomes alive.

There is no contradiction between Saint John Chrysostom and Saint Ignatius Brianchaninov and Saint Symeon the New Theologian: **To not fill yourself with the spirit of vanity means to be humble.** And on the contrary, to fill yourself up with the spirit of vanity means to ascend above with your heart, it means pride. Moreover, longing for vanities means to want to ascend above others or even God with your heart.

Saint Basil the Great says: "Close is the Almighty to those with broken hearts, and he will save those humble in spirit. **A broken heart means the destruction of human thoughts.** He who despises the things down here and surrenders himself to the Word of God, he who offers the ruling power of his soul to the thoughts above man and the divine; he is the one with the broken heart and makes in his heart a sacrifice that God will not despise. *The sacrifices of God are a broken spirit, a broken and a contrite heart-- These, O God, You will not despise* (Psalm 51:17). God is, therefore, close to those with a broken heart and He will save those who are humble in spirit. He who is not conceited and does not think of anything worldly, this one is broken in heart and humble in spirit".

Saint John Chrysostom says the same: "**There is no other way for someone to become humble**, only through the love for God and for holiness **and by despising worldly things**".

To be poor in spirit means to be humble, says Saint John Chrysostom, but he goes further and says that nobody can be humble unless he despises worldly things. How could he despise them, if he is full of them? If he is full of their spirit? Only if he is poor in these spirits with a small "*s*", different worldly spirits, spirits of vanity, he will be humble. Otherwise, it is impossible. You say you love worldly culture (namely poetry, literature, science) but are you humble? It's not possible. You say you listen to lay music, you watch TV, you go to the theater and concerts, and you are humble? This is not possible. No, no, you are in delusion, you flatter yourself, you feign godliness. You are a football fan, but you are humble? It's not possible. You cannot be an admirer of a sport star, music, theater or movie star if you are humble. Only if you are proud, says Saint John Chrysostom. You admire them, only if you want to be like them, only if you value the world, and you do not believe or value the glory of God and the Kingdom of Heaven.

We often hear: What, don't I deserve this? Why shouldn't I have this? How many of the purchases you have made are really necessary? And how many are made so that you can keep up with others? Or how many are made purely because of pride, in wanting to have something special which will tell the whole world: see this shiny car, I, its owner, am the same. No doubt many **people imagine that a part of the glory of their civilization is transferred unto them**. And that is why they will not be able to give up so easily something related to civilization: they love evanescent glory. The doors open by themselves in front of them, the remote control beeps pleasantly, the lights are flashing. How is this not to worship them?

Saint Basil the Great, in his word *On humility,* says: "If the man had remained in the glory ordained for him by God, he wouldn't have had false greatness, but a real one. That's why, the best way to his salvation, to cure his disease and return to the initial condition, is humility, namely he should not imagine that he can adorn himself by his own powers with any kind of glory. But the devil, which took down man with the hope of a false glory, does not stop luring with the same temptations and contrives many schemes for this".

When someone watches a movie, he participates in the actors' success. He imagines that part of the actor's cleverness, power, beauty, youth and success transfers to him when in fact he is filled with pride and the spirit of vanity. He becomes connected with the actor's words which seem so important in the movie. Somehow he is connected with the luxury he watches there or the movie's adventures. The actors seem to be on the stage, but actually, those who watch them are on the stage and imagine that they do wonderful things. The singers seem to sing, but in fact, those who listen to them are singing spiritually; they sing haughty songs in defiance of God, in defiance of Christ's commandments. In this way, they create a parallel world animated by the spirit of vanity, created by pride and imagination. Satan ascended to the skies, wanted to place his throne above God and by some mysterious way, he attracted the other angels too, who became demons. The same thing will happen to those who drink from the demonic spirit of vanity, their hearts will rise and ascend above, but they are actually attracted and deceived by the devil away from God.

Saint .John of Kronstadt says: To him who is poor in spirit the whole world is as nothing.

Chapter 3

The Angels' Fall

How did a third of the Angels fall?

It is very useful for us to understand how we are deceived, how our proto-parents were deceived and how the fallen angels were attracted. We know that Satan took pride, but how did, up to a third of the angels fall with him? And if angels could be tempted, how can we not be?

No doubt demonic deception is not always something which is obvious to everybody, and it does not deceive only little children. All people are in deception, specifies Saint Ignatius Brianchaninov. But how is it that the angels were attracted into this deception?

Saint Symeon the New Theologian: says about someone summoned by the King "if you were to turn your face, that means your mind is somewhere else and you will talk or have a conversation with another, namely turning your back to unapproachable God, where the heavenly armies look without blinking with fear and quiver, wouldn't it rightfully leave you as contemptuous and unworthy? ...But if you consider as nothing His love and sweetness, then you will be inclined to the love of another. You will connect the whole soul's activity to this, and you will find pleasure in nothing else, than food or drinks, or seductive clothes or views, gold or silver or you will engrave inside your soul the image of another passion. Will then, The Clean One and immaculate, Who bore you in Spirit, accept to be with you, who consented to all this or will He not rather leave you? It is obvious to anyone".

Similarly, we think about the dark angels' fall. Amazed by the fallen cherub, Satan, they turned their faces to look at him, and they delighted with his show, message, ideology, and spirit.

It is not easy to believe that so many angels who fell together had no common cause, a source of delusion that they looked to or that they did not look one to another, and they fell independently. In the life of Saint Niphon of Constantia there appears the following fragment: Once after prayer, the Saint was in a state of spiritual ecstasy and saw a broad field, equal in width and length, and on it stood a multitude of Ethiopians, divided into regiments; there were 365 regiments in all, according to the number of the most serious sins. One of the darkest Ethiopians counted the warriors, arranging the regiments as if for battle, and said: **Look at me** and do no fear anything; my power will be with you!

The same today the demons and the vain people look to Satan and to his things and take their power from there. We cannot deny that the Holy Bible suggests a sequence of events: First Satan took pride and elevated himself and did other things that the Holy Bible does not specify; perhaps in order to not harm the reader. And then, one-third of all the angels fell; most probably because they turned their eyes to Satan, having been attracted by his show. Then they turned from God and ceased glorifying Him. Blessed Andrew, the Fool for Christ, says that Satan: "Fell because he envied the glory of God and **thought to establish a kingdom of his own together with the other forsaken angels**".

What kind of a kingdom did he want to establish? How did Satan present it to the fallen angels? How was this grand show? Didn't it offer a sort of joy and fulfillment? Didn't it surprise, overwhelm and irresistibly attract?

In contemporary language, we can imagine it as a grand show, of music and lights, as an artistic masterpiece, as a fascinating poem and an overflow of scientific discoveries setting in motion a brilliant technology, like a giant 3-D game.

We should not forget for a single moment that **getting filled up and sharing in this illusion is pride**.

This spirit of vanity fell on the earth with Satan and has accompanied mankind with its delusions until this day. **It discovered itself gradually, as much as God allowed it**, because otherwise, it would have scorched everything around.

But, towards the end of the world when Satan will be untied, this spirit will work with extreme power in the world: *He must be released for a little while* (Revelation 20, 3).

If before the fall the angels just like clean mirrors (as Saint Symeon the New Theologian says) reflected the light of God then by their own will they turned to reflect something else and reflected the spirit of Satan. And this spirit of delusion rolled down from heaven and is found on the earth, acts in the world, blinding and killing men's souls.

Therefore, when you leave home, you should expect to find something from the works of the fallen cherub, astonishing works like those that led to the fall of the forsaken angels from heaven. Be careful not to share, delight and get drunk on these delusions!

When you go to work, when you turn on the TV or meet someone you should expect to find again works of the fallen cherub.

Saint Antony the Great said: I saw all the traps that the enemy spreads out over the world, and I said groaning: Who can get through such snares?

The spirit that works inside these snares is the same with the spirit that led to the fall of the forsaken angels, as the Holy Spirit is one, but the gifts are many, so it is with the spirit of vanity, which led to the fall of the deceived angels, and now leads to the fall of people, even if it is not identical in the form of a manifestation, yet it is closely related, having the same source and spring. What kind of water flows from this spring? This spirit is the spirit of lie and delusion, says Saint Ignatius Brianchaninov.

The worldly spirit is that seductive magic, which could transform angels into devils, and now it distracts people from their way to heaven directing them towards hell. It is the spirit: *in which you once walked according to the course of this world, according to the prince of the power of the air, the spirit who now works in the sons of disobedience* (Ephesians 2: 2).

By whom people are attracted

We can see that there is a spirit of this world, namely the worldly spirit, which is according to the master of the air under the sky, namely the devil and that it works in the children of disobedience, namely in the devils and worldly people, even if in different ways.

Do you think that nowadays celebrities are delightful, and the heroes in the movies do not match with the Gospel? But the fallen cherub was much more brilliant and attractive and afterward he became frightful, ugly and evil. Do you admire, or are you captivated by the charms or success of worldly men, professional athletes, great scientists, or famous artists and does this distract you from God? If so, remember that the fallen cherub does his work of deception through these people. Turning you away from contemplating the heavenly ones is already a great victory for him, it is your fall or the beginning of your fall.

Saint John of Kronstadt says: "O, how carefully do the devil and the world sow their tares in Christ's cornfield, which is the Church of God. Instead of the Word of God, the word of the world, the word of vanity, is shown. Instead of the temple of God, the world has invented its own temples, the temples of the world's vanities: theaters, circuses, assemblies. Instead of holy icons, which worldly people do not accept, in the world, there are painted and photographic portraits, illustrations, and various other pictures. Instead of God and the Saints, the world honors unto adoration its own celebrities: writers, actors, singers, painters, who command general confidence and respect up to reverence. Poor Christians! They have completely fallen away from Christ! Instead of spiritual raiment, every attention is paid in the world to perishable clothing, to fashionable dresses, and various exquisite ornaments, both splendid and costly".

What does it mean that Satan will be released from the depths toward the end of the world? It means that his spirit will manifest itself with uncommon power in the world. With similar power, perhaps, to that which led to the fall of one-third of all the angels, and which made them stop glorifying God and turn their eyes to Satan and his works.

The remedy is given for man in antiquity as well as for contemporary man by The Holy Apostle Paul in First Epistle to the Corinthians: *Those who rejoice should be as thought they did not rejoice, those who buy as they did not possess and those who use this world as not misusing it* (7:29-30). Namely, not to fill themselves up with the spirit of vanity, not to be delighted by things surrounding him, not to attach to the creation more than the Creator.

He who knows God hears us; he who is not of God does not hear us. By this we know the spirit of truth and the spirit of error (1 John 4:6) says Saint John the Evangelist. This spirit of error attracted man angels toward falling and dominated them. It exerted a strong, very strong attraction. No wonder that people are attracted and directed since even a part of the angels fell. *It is the spirit which manifests in the world through the lust of the flesh, the lust of the eyes and the pride of life* (1 John 2:16). Nobody can resist it, unless it is born from above and then he can fall anytime, just like those fallen angels. Yes, the seductive music, shows, movies, special effects, animations, explosions of light and color are fragments of the spirit which caused the angels to crash down. The luxurious buildings, worldly science and technology and culture are a way by which (those driven by the worldly spirit) say with the originator of evil: *I will ascend above the heights of the clouds, I will be like the Most High* (Isaiah 14:14).

In the same way as guarding against the spirit of vanity, which tries to intoxicate hearts, means humility and poorness in spirit, so too if you let yourself ride on the waves of this spirit it clearly means pride, and pride is inseparable from this spirit of vanity.

If the spirit of vanity works powerfully, it banishes grace, and without the grace of the Holy Spirit, man cannot defend himself from any sin. Saint John of Kronstadt says: Unless the Holy Spirit strengthens our soul, it is constantly inclined to every sin, and, therefore, to spiritual death.

The devil who was haughty was amazed by this vain spirit produced by his bright mind, spirit and illusion, which delighted and amazed and attracted irresistibly other angels wherafter they were no longer secondary lights of God, but reflections of this haughty and vain illusion, which was nevertheless brilliant and attractive in a certain way.

It is unimaginable the glamour and the power of this illusion, which was able to attract into fall a lot of angels. Taken by surprise, a lot of angels were attracted to it. Of course, it manifests itself on the earth too, but much weaker than it could and did in the world of spirits. It manifests on earth as much as God allows it. Shows, music, fireworks, brilliant shop windows, drunkenness of the senses by refined methods, may suggest what happened (when the third part of the angels fell) and what may happen at the end of the world with almost all mankind. All these refined entertainments are directed and orchestrated by the demons with the help of the vessels full of the cunning spirit: movie stars, singers, politicians, and other personalities of the moment.

Gradual meeting with the Spirit of Vanity

Mankind could not have endured the sudden meeting with this spirit of vanity in all its power, so it was revealed gradually and will attain towards the end a power somewhat close to what made the angels fall from heaven. Who can resist the confrontation with these powers? This is what Saint Ephraim the Syrian wonders: Who will really have a soul as strong as a diamond to be able to bravely suffer all those temptations? What man can resist where the angels fell? Certainly not lukewarm believers, pampered Christians, grown up in luxury and amusement who spend their time listening to music and watching TV, who are bound by hundreds of wires to modern civilization.

Mankind became acquainted with the spirit of vanity gradually so that the true Christians might get accustomed to it slowly in order to be able to fight against it. Who would dare to say that these are only innocent pleasures? Of course, most of them made enrichment with the spirit of vanity the very purpose of their lives. Their placement in hell is not sudden as it was with the demons but it is delayed until the end of earthly life, due to the mercy of God. (But, God will pick up with His wisdom some of them out from the whirlpool of vanity and by a miracle He will lead them to the Kingdom of heaven).

Saint Ignatius Brianchaninov says: "The ruler of this world strives to keep us in endless amusement and darkness by means of the pleasures of the flesh! Through the bodily senses, the very windows to the soul through which it has a connection with the visible world, it feeds unceasingly the delights of the senses, and at the same time also with sin and the slavery which are inseparable from it. In the famous earthly concert halls sounds a music which expresses and stirs various passions; these passions are also represented in earthly theaters; these passions are stirred by earthly amusement: man is brought by any means to the delight with the evil that kills him. Drugging himself with it, they forget about God and the blood of God - Man by which we were ransomed".

Even if the spirit that attracted the angels to fall is not identical in its manifestation with the worldly spirit which attracts people, yet they are closely related since they have the same source: Satan.

He who is accustomed to this spirit of vanity will look for it in the spiritual life, will try to fill himself with it when praying, even by looking at Holy Icons, listening to church services or visiting churches and monasteries.

At the end of the world, the Antichrist will try to remake that grand show, that magic which led to the angels' fall. That irresistible attraction which made the third part of angels fall will manifest (probably with the help of technology) to a great extent over mankind. And we must see that we have already started to live those times. Man cannot resist being attracted by this flood of the world. We should not be surprised that almost all of us have already fallen under the sway of technology.

If you see someone turning off the road to the left, you shout to him to take to the right. Of course, this urge is not meant for those who go straight or who go off the road, but going more to the right. In general, I think that no matter how much we would try, practically in our lives, to fight technology, we will still be inclined and attracted to use in excess the technological developments and various facilities and modern things and give them an undeserved place in our hearts.

It is becoming more clear that technology, science and worldly culture will be that delusion which will fool even the chosen ones. We must be sincere and observe technology (and science and culture) according to their fruits. How does it help in our prayers the fact that we have a stronger computer? Does it help us to be more merciful? Does it help us in the work of any virtue? It is possible to find cases when it seems that it helps. But something is wrong.

We must observe technology according to its fruits. I don't like those who say that technology is not bad. It is as if you would go to a diabetes ward in a hospital and you would say that sugar is not bad by itself. And you would start to explain the metabolic processes it participates in and how it generates energy and so on. All true. But if they listen to this, they will die. Whoever says that technology is not bad wants to justify himself. Instead of recognizing (so that he might improve) that technology penetrated into our lives and that we must strive to stop it, otherwise, it will lead us away from Christ.

Sugar is not bad, but it is bad for diabetics. The same goes for us with technology. Spiritually, it is not good. It doesn't matter whether because of it or because of us. If there are people who are not affected by technology, I do not argue with them. We answer to such people the following: *Those who are well have no need of a doctor, but those who are sick* (Luke 5:31). Those who say that technology is not bad, that they are in good health should not receive such cures (meant for sick people like me). We do not argue with them and do not want to demonstrate anything to them. What would there be to demonstrate when everything is so clear around us?

Wealth and technology are not bad by themselves. It's true. The same with food, it is not bad. Yet, for a diabetic sugar is bad, for a kidney disease or a hypertensive salt is not good, for a liver disease fat is not good. You don't go to an alcoholic and say that it is not bad to drink a glass of wine at lunch. Wealth and technology are not bad for a healthy man spiritually (who maintained his health just because he protected himself from the harmful things) not for sick people like us. For most of us, these (technology, science, worldly culture) do nothing but feed passions.

Blessed Theophylact of Ochrid says: "It is impossible not to use badly what we have; that until we have wealth, the devil strives to deceive us, to use it sometimes far from the common rules, and it is hard to escape from his snares. For that, poverty is a good thing and almost without any temptation".

The Spirit of Vanity attracted some of the Holy Apostle Paul's Disciples

No doubt that the spirit of vanity works very powerfully and the lure of the worldly vanities over people is very strong. Just think what, the holy Apostle Paul says about one of his disciples: *has forsaken me, having loved this present world, and has departed* (2 Timothy 4:10). Even the Apostle Paul could not stop them from jumping into the stream of vanity. *Do not love the world or the things in the world* (1 John 2:15) shouts Saint John the Evangelist. And The Holy Apostle Paul explains: *For the grace of God that brings salvation has appeared to all men, teaching us denying ungodliness and worldly lusts* (Titus 2:11-12) and adds *For we ourselves were also once foolish, disobedient, deceived, serving various lusts and pleasures* (Titus 3:3).

In the book of *Revelation* it is written that an angel: *laid hold of the dragon, the serpent of old, who is the Devil and Satan, and bound him for a thousand years; and he cast him into the bottomless pit, and shut him up, and set a seal on him, so that he should deceive the nations no more till the thousand years were finished. But after this things, he must be released for a little while* (20:2-3). It means that now he is released or will be soon, and deceives people with civilization and technology, Oriental practices, television and the internet, concerts, films, music, lights and magic. And all of these are alike, vain and soul-killing things, which make man unable to turn his eyes to God and to stick to the earth. He deceived long ago, but how did he had deceived then and how does he deceive now?! We read further: *Woe to the inhabitants of the earth and the sea! For the devil has come down to you, having great wrath, because he knows that he has a short time* (Revelation 12:12) has come down with delusions, music and light shows, with magic, with all glamour that may attract man from serving God.

The Fall of Angels and the Fall of Men

Saint Ignatius Brianchaninov writes that the other fallen angels "were involved in this haughtiness and blindness by one of the angelic leaders". How exactly? By what means? By means similar to those with which people are deceived? Bishop Ignatius says: "They (fallen spirits) under the leadership of their chief, tried to seduce man, to involve him in their own fall, to turn him into an obedient companion, to infect him with the poison of their hatred against God, which they did".

"Condemned to crawl on the earth, the fallen angel does its best that man to do the same thing. Man is also inclined to this, due to the blindness by which he was affected. Of course, man has the sense of eternity, but due to the fact that this sense is perverted by what is unfairly called intellect and by its slumbering conscience, it seems to him that earthly life is endless too. Relying on this seductive impression, but illusory and disastrous, man is enslaved by the work and occupations which provide a comfortable life for him, forgetting that he is a traveler and that his permanent house is either in heaven or in hell. In the name of fallen man, Holy Scripture cries out to God: *my soul clings to the dust; Revive me according to Your word.* (Ps. 119:25). It is clear that the attachment to the earth hits the soul with eternal death; he is restored to life by the word of God, which pulls him off the ground and raises his thoughts and feelings to heaven.

"The devil", says Saint John Chrysostom, "is wicked. He attacks from below. And in this case, wins for sure because we do not try to rise up to where he cannot hurt us anymore. If you don't know what it means to be attacked from below, allow me to explain this method of fighting. It consists in defeating by using earthly realities, pleasures, wealth and everything that is in the world. That is why the devil when he sees someone ascending high spiritually, first is unable to attack him and if he risks doing that, he will fall himself. Do not fear him, because he has no wings, but he only crawls on the earth, among earthly things. Is better to have nothing in common with him, because in this case, the effort is not necessary". "Earthly concerns when the monk is dedicated enthusiastically to them, may, without causing him to commit any express sins, stop him from spiritual growth and cause disaster in his soul". "Intellectual concerns, in particular, risk to drive man away from humility and God and involve him in self-confidence and idolizing his own person".

"If man during the earthly journey does not break any connection with the spirits of evil, he will remain tied to them, even after his death, belonging to them more or less, depending to what extent he was in touch with them. Maintaining the connection with the fallen spirits may lead to eternal damnation when an incomplete break causes terrible pains on the way to heaven. Look, brothers, what the devil did and is doing is to remove the thought of man away from spiritual heaven towards the material world, enslaving the heart of the earth and earthly occupations ... The fallen spirit convinced many monks to obtain various rare and precious objects, and when their thought clung to these objects, they separated them from God. It made others study all kinds of sciences and arts, of minor importance which might direct them toward earth; and when it captivated their attention with ephemeral knowledge, it deprived them of necessary knowledge, that about God". These tactics of binding to the earth "is so practical in leading man to destruction, that these days the Evil One will use them to separate the whole world from God. The devil uses this kind of fight with incontestable success. These days, under the influence of the lord of this world, man will be literally possessed by attachment to earth and to all that is material and bodily. They will be possessed by the worries of this world and will be concerned with the development of material assets. They will take care exclusively of developing land as if they had their eternal home here. Becoming bodily and material, they will forget about eternity as if it didn't exist; they will forget about God and will leave Him".

What a big mystery is the fall of the forsaken angels. We understand why Satan fell. But, what about the other angels? How was it possible that so many angels be deceived by Satan?

We all know that those who had a vision of or by some other means visited heaven came back totally changed and despised entirely earthly things, such as the brother of the king in the life of the Apostle Thomas. (It is probable that God might have somehow withdrawn grace from them for a while, to see where their will goes, as Saint Silouan teaches about the withdrawal of grace that sometimes occurs in saints' lives.)

What delusions did Satan use to attract the angels? Why did so many angels fall? How many men would resist if he were allowed to spread his delusions on earth? But, in the end times he will be untied. Not entirely, but to a great extent. Imagination, science, technology, comfort, luxury and good living will fashion a life that will seem without grace although to some of the chosen ones, extremely attractive. The man without grace will be attracted and subjugated with irresistible force.

Imagination and Pride

Archimandrite Sophrony writes: "**Pride amplifies imagination**, humility makes it stop. Pride rises above, creating its own world. Pride united with imagination made the devil fall, and he wants to pull us down in the same way". An extreme manifestation of pride was accompanied, probably, by an extreme manifestation of imagination so spectacular, that it surprised the angels causing them to fall. The fallen angels were attracted by the dream like a grand show of Satan. Any manifestation of vain glory is ugly in front of God. God stands against the proud ones, and He gives grace to the humble. Satan fell like a lightning flash and since then he seeks to paint dreams and shows in human minds. His dreams lift them and fill them with pride and the spirit of vanity. *You will be like God* (Genesis 3, 5) is the dream of dreams and the fall of falls. "Dreaming, yet alluring and beautiful in appearance for the simple fact that it is an abusive and arbitrary composition of the mind, pulls the mind away from the state of divine truth, bringing it to the state of self-deception and delusion. That is why it should be abandoned", writes Saint Ignatius Brianchaninov.

Saint Nicodemus of the Holy Mountain says: "Find out that he who was Lucifer, the first among angels, at first was above this irrational imagination. Then imagining and reckoning his mind equal to God, fell in this very divided, rough and multiform imagination. That is why he is called by the Holy Fathers a painter of all, an imitator and a snake with many faces, an eater of the earth's passions, an illusion, and other such names. So, learn from this, dear, **that various forms of imagination as they are an invention and illusion of devil, they are very desirable to him**. Because according to some saints, imagination is the bridge where the deadly demons pass by and mingle in the soul and so make an abode for bad, ugly, opprobrious thoughts and of all unclean passions for soul and body ... You should know that according to Saint Maximus the Confessor, **Adam was created without imagination**. His mind was clean, uniform, stable, in the same activity. That is why he did not imagine anything, was not a slave of his senses and forms of things that are driven by the senses. So, from that rational, angelical, uniform, unitary and steadfast life was thrown away by the devil into perceivable, multilateral and unsteady imagination and in the state of being like the irrational animals. As imagination is a feature of irrational animals, not of the rational ones. Once man fell into such a state, who can say how many passions, how much viciousness, and what errors he was thrown into? (Run away from any imagination and memorial of good or bad things because all these are impurities and filthiness, which darkens the mind's cleanliness, nobleness, and brilliance). There is no bodily or soul passion that might come to the mind by any other way than by imagination. So, strive to maintain your mind clean, without forms, colors, distances and any fantasy, as God created it!"

The Source of the Spirit of Vanity

Saint Gregory Palamas writes: "So as if God is the life-giving goodness of the living no doubt that the devil is **a dead and death-giving evil**". "Thus, he becomes a dead spirit, not through being, but by casting off true life. But, unrestrained in his inclination to evil and enhancing it with extreme wickedness makes himself **a death-giving spirit, striving to attract man to his death**". "Satan wanted to rule with haughtiness against the decision of the Creator. Thus, he deceived or better said persuaded people not to consider and not to give any value, even to disregard and to oppose and to create contrary teachings against the advice given by the Most Good. **Thus, sharing his rebellion, people share also his darkness and eternal death**". So, the proto-parents of mankind "uniting in thought with the dead spirit of Satan and eating from the forbidden tree, against the will of the Creator have stripped off their bright clothes and the brightness of life-giving from above and made themselves dead in spirit, like Satan. And, Satan is not only a dead spirit but a death-giving spirit for those who approach him. But those who shared in his death also had a body, through which was accomplished in deed the death-giving advice, so this death passes on to their bodies together with the death-giving spirit of evil".

"But Satan wanted to rule against the decision of the Creator"- and wanted to attract other angels just like today he wants to attract other people. For this, he used all his special powers, all his arguments, supported by delightful lies and convincing imaginations similar to modern advertising clips, but much more enhanced by a frightful power of attraction, which made even angels fall. (Angel's fall and man's fall are similar in that they relate to the spirit; in other words, coming from the same death-giving spirit. Just like a part bears the imprint of the whole, we may assume that the partial work of the devil developed on earth today is from the same spirit which deceived the fallen angels, but on a much smaller scale- as much as God allows on earth.) These imaginations were similar to the modern advertising clips, shows in stadiums, hallucinating animations made today by means of the computer, and they were inducing a state of well-being and fascination.

The fall of the angels is a great mystery. And it starts to reveal to some extent while civilization and technology advance enabling the implementation of the most fantastic imaginations, by creating some imagined worlds, by living and experimenting ever stronger states of amazement. At the end, the devil *must be released* as it is written in Revelation (20:3). It means that he will act on earth as never before, and we can see that he does it on the earth in an unimaginable way until recently. We don't know where this way of life will lead, but we can see that it comes more and more to an astonishing show where Satan handles like a puppeteer the people who surrendered and are surrendering to him by their own will. But he will have no power over those who look towards the light of Christ, the salvation and the Savior of the world from the deception of the cunning one.

Due to technological progress in audiovisual systems and the use of the special software, we can suppose the extent of the illusions which were used in that battle when a multitude of angels fell. But they surpass even the most amazing and terrible imaginations. In a similar way, multitudes of people, potential saints, are deceived by the works developed by Satan on earth.

In the Philokalia, Hesychius of Sinai writes: "Just like a small child without malice, seeing a magician perform, will be delighted and will follow him, with innocence, our soul delighted and deceived with the devil's illusions runs towards evil like to someone good". The spirit of vanity acts over people in the same way that it acted over the fallen angels.

Saint Ignatius Brianchaninov says: "Binding to the material world and to material wealth may easily absorb man in his entirety, his mind, his heart, may deprive him of all his time and powers: *because of the fall my soul clings to the dust* (Ps.119:25) ...*If anyone loves the world*, (namely earthly life with its enhancement and delight), preached to all people the Holy Spirit of God *the love of the Father is not in him* (1 John 2:15). *Friendship with the world is enmity with God. Whoever therefore wants to be a friend of the world makes himself an enemy of God* (James. 4:4). *You cannot serve God and mammon*, namely being in service to God and to earthly growth (Matthew 6:24)".

"And the new Israel (Christians) will forsake, according to the testimony of the Holy Bible, its spiritual worthiness, already given by the Redeemer, for the purpose of earthly growth, easily evanescent, the growth supposed only in deceived dreaming, and will defame the Holy Spirit preferring its fallen intellect with a deceitful name. The old Israel was deceived by dreaming of high earthly wealth, the new Israel will be deceived by the same kind of dreaming and the same aspiration." "Most of the people, *giving heed to deceiving spirits and doctrines of demons* (1 Timothy. 4:1), going crazy because of the action of this teaching over them, despised the Word of God, and they don't know and would not want to know about it."

The Kingdom of Satan is shadow and lie

Saint John of Kronstadt notices: "but in the Devil, who fell away from God, only a shadow of thought remains, and his word is without truth, without the reality of the deed--a lie, a phantom; and as a truthful word, being an image of God the Word, and being derived from Him, is life, so the lying word of the Devil, being his image, is death. Falsehood is necessarily death, for the death of the soul is naturally caused by that which has itself fallen from life into death". "From the Devil, who fell through his pride, who wished to appropriate to himself the impossible, and who fell away from life and truth, come illusion, falsehood, and death from death". "Attachment to earthly and carnal things to the oblivion of God, of the soul, proceeds from the Devil, who, through attachment to earthly things, makes our heart carnal, earthly, a shameful vessel of passions, whilst it ought to be meditating upon heavenly things, to be spiritual and the temple of the Holy Spirit".

Probably, the fallen angels were wrong in the same way, letting themselves be delighted by Satan instead of looking up to God, they looked towards the discoveries, imaginations, games and this attractive and haughty show offered by Satan. We cannot serve both God and mammon. It was first valid for the fallen angels. And we repeat now, just like then: *Let us be steadfast, let us stay with fear, let us take heed*, because the discoveries, illusions, fireworks, music and other similar things will overflow at the end with a power close to that which made some of the angels turn their eyes away from God. Then, who will be able not to be attracted by the amazing discoveries of science, hallucinating shows, games, contests, advertising and entertainment, all meant to turn the eyes of everybody away from God to something else?

Saint Tikhon of Zadonsk notices: "Every man is between God and the world, between time and eternity, as between heaven and earth. When he turns to the world and loves it, then he turns away from God and does not love Him. Because Apostle John says: *If anyone loves the world, the love of the Father is not in him* (1 John 2:15). When you care about the ephemeral things, you forget about the eternal ones, just like when you turn your face and eyes to earth, you turn them away from heaven. **When you think of time, you forget about eternity**"...

Chapter 4

Living people and dead people

How will I find out whether I am alive?

The following matter is brought into question: What spirit am I being guided by? Am I dead, or am I alive? Is what *The Book of Revelation* tells us valid for me as well (3, 1): *"I know your works, that you have a name that you are alive, but you are dead"*? Or what was said to the widow: *who lives in pleasure is dead while she lives* (1Timothy 5, 6)? When am I dead, and when am I alive? When am I brought back to life, and how do I know that I have been raised?

These questions may have the following answer: When your conscience rebukes you, when you have zeal, you are on the narrow path and you are alive. Saint John Chrysostom pointed out: "There is within us a flame that burns eternally and that is called inner voice or **conscience**. If the evil spirit comes inside in a hurry and extinguishes that flame, then the soul will have immediately been darkened and taken down and suddenly deprived of everything within."

Saint Theophan the Recluse teaches about the remorse of conscience: "First of all, **the grace teaches man to unmask himself and take off all his coatings:** thus, how would it be possible to work without seeing what exactly you have to work on? In **this work blindness disappears from the eyes of the mind**, the heart feels again and the will wakes up from the indifference where it slept. The tree without leaves of the sin is now being perceived by the sinner's eyes of the mind, in all its hideous emptiness and now — something which is unusual to him — bears self-reproach, covers with shame, burns with accusatory judgment and with remorse of conscience." One of the prophecies of Saint Nilus the Myrrhstreamer on the end of the world: "Due to the power of such great sins, people are going to be deprived of the grace of the Holy Spirit which they received at the Holy Baptism, as well as remorse of conscience."

There are some people who seem to have no conscience. Actually, what's the matter with them? All of them, as The Holy Fathers teach us, have their soul dead, dying, or numb. The light from their souls turned off. They are blind and, therefore, will fall into the abyss. However, they can become saints, they can wake up, enlighten, and find the way. Do you have remorse of conscience because you did not pray that you are immersed in the material ones and that you have forgotten Jesus Christ? Yes or no, according to the state of your soul. In the same time, with the man's development, the development of the conscience takes place.

In order to be able to guide himself, the Christian has to listen to the **voice of conscience and if he has no conscience anymore, to guide himself following the voice of the conscience of others**. By reading The Lives of the Saints and Fathers of the Church, the Christian searches for similar situations with his own and sees the guidance given by the Saints' consciences, as they are the ones whose conscience is alive and working and who experienced similar situations.

Having no conscience is not an insult but a reality of our contemporary world. Multitudes of people notice the very same fact: they have no conscience anymore. This is, as I have already pointed out, the evidence that their soul is dead or almost dead. We may no longer feel any remorse of conscience when we don't go to church, we don't fast, when we are not giving alms, and when we commit big and heavy sins.

It is of utmost importance for any Christian to understand what happens with our soul when we no longer feel any remorse of conscience...

On the other hand, the work of the conscience became extremely surprisingly and astonishing, nowadays, as the proof of the souled death, which is all over. Yet, we are even more surprised by the sharpened conscience of the Saints.

The work of the conscience seen in others rejoices and brightens up the soul mysteriously, helping it to get rid of the tyranny of the evil and despondency.

Art, culture, and the entire worldly wisdom usually **make up a distinct world without conscience.** This bewildering spectacle of the science and art is unceasingly revealed in front of astonished eyes of the Christians and has, amongst other**, the effect of the sleeping of the conscience**. Meanwhile, there are promoted other consciences: the civic conscience, national one, professional one, so that there is remaining only little place for that conscience planted within man by God to lead him to holiness.

Spiritual Conscience

The spiritual conscience is not the same as that particular bodily conscience, which springs from the teachings of the minds. The spiritual conscience rebukes us for the spiritual ones, while the bodily one rebukes us for bodily ones. The spiritual conscience belongs to the souls, while the bodily one belongs to the body. Sometimes, they may mix, and it is more difficult to set them apart, or they may even work together for a while. However, spiritual conscience leads to fear of God and piety, while bodily conscience leads to despise the spiritual ones. It leads us to pride, self-sufficiency and tightly connects us to the material ones. The bodily conscience is a sort of perfectionism, meaning to do all your best to become a good professional, a trustful citizen of this earthly world. It helps you find your place on earth but obstructs you to find it in heaven. This may create the false feeling that someone is not dead, while in fact, it is an ephemeral replacement of spiritual conscience and must work as its devoted servant, one that is always ready to help when it is wounded not to fight with it.

The spiritual conscience also urges us to bodily, worldly, social deeds but, first and foremost, urges us to spiritual deeds. Yet, **this worldly, bodily conscience means a true absence of spiritual conscience**, as Saint Symeon the New Theologian similarly point out when talking about the worldly wisdom: "So, this worldly knowledge is, no doubts, an ignorance of anything good; because, if it had not fallen from the true knowledge and seeing of God, it would not have fallen to such knowledge." In the same way, we may say that this bodily conscience is a true lack of conscience, since if man had not fallen from spiritual conscience, would not have fallen to such bodily conscience, to this rightness and worldly moral.

Saint Ignatius Brianchaninov dedicates an entire chapter to the conscience: "The Teaching of Jesus Christ, sealed by the Holy Baptism, **heals the conscience of the cunningness that the sin infected it with** …Sins that are committed willingly darken, choke and numb conscience...the conscience that is enlightened and sharpened by the Gospel shows man, in detail and clearly, all his mistakes, to the most insignificant ones." Yet, the conscience will show the path to be followed to heal his soul; otherwise, the man would fall into despair.

On those with numb conscience, he said: "Finally callousness becomes the usual state of the soul. The soul is often pleased with it; more often than not it considers that this state is pleasant to God, peace of conscience, while it actually means that soul loses the perception of the sins, loss of any feeling of the grace and spiritual life, sleep and blindness of the conscience."

"The conscience don't judge only those who are on the top of the virtue or sin." Therefore, between carnal people and the spiritual ones, there are some similarities concerning the remorse of conscience. The spiritual one feels less remorse, because they have the peace of Jesus Christ, while the carnal ones do not feel remorse of conscience because their soul is dead. **From outside, they seem to be similar.**

Not having spiritual conscience is not an insult; it is a reality we must fight with, it is the starting point. Saint Paisios of Mount Athos calls it the good worry and talks about it frequently.

Saint Ignatius Brianchaninov points out: "The **state of health** of the **conscience is** possible only inside the Orthodox Church."

Saint Theophan the Recluse wrote: "Keep in mind: whenever you are utterly unsatisfied with yourself, you are good state; as soon as is coming a slightest feeling of self-satisfaction and you start appreciating yourself, you need to know that you are not in your usual state and you should start rebuke yourself...The t**riumph in spiritual life is shown by the greater and greater conscience of our nothingness in the most strict sense of this word, without any limitation**...As sinner you will feel that you are, as more strait your spiritual path will be. But you must get there, so that the feeling of your sinfulness to come naturally from the deep of your soul, not to be inspired from outside, by your mind or somebody else's words."

Besides the conscience, Saint Theophan the Recluse reveals another two signs that shows if the soul is alive: **thirst for God** and the **fear of God**.

People who act and people who react

Thus, there are two types of people, some who act and others who react. The living people act and the dead ones react. These ones react to temptations, lures, pushes, advices, whispers, and the illusions of the devil. The devil shows them beads and coloured glasses, which have images of luxury cars, money, houses, pleasures, worldly fame, and uncleanliness. And people run for these coloured beads. And the sign that they are in such a state is that, in the absence of the coloured beads, man is inert, just as a puppet fallen down; he feels that life is meaningless, is not in mood for anything, expecting the temptations that are the ones that make alive any man who is spiritually dead.

But, actually what should be the state of those who act, who do not run for devils' beads, but are free and alive in Christ, shaded by the grace of the Holy Spirit? People who live indeed and act in order to get closer to God, the real life, as He Himself confessed: *"I am the way, the truth, and the life"* (John 14, 6) and again *"Unless you eat the flesh of the Son of Man and drink his blood, you have no life in you"* (John 6, 53). Once the soul is alive, it acts to get closer to God, but once it is dead, it is pushed away from God.

Holy Fathers divide people in three states of the soul: the dead, the living, and those who have not the soul entirely dead. The last are either dead who came back to life (by repentance and with the help of Holy Spirit) or living people whose souls started to die (due to their carelessness or sins).

Saint Theophan the Recluse writes: "We cannot serve both God and Mammon. Divided minds and divided hearts make the man useless, since *anyone whose mind is divided is unstable in all his ways.* He will do either nothing, or builds with one hand and destroys with the other."

Hence, we understand that there are two types of stable people: some who determinedly serve God and others who determinedly serve Mammon. Some are full of Holy Spirit and other of the spirit of vanity.

The unfaithful ones are like a leaf on the wind, says The Apostle, rainless clouds. But, we see that many unfaithful have on the contrary, grow, confidence, wealth, and worldly power. What should be this? This means that they are faithful not unfaithful, but in Satan, or his ideas and his works, and they are full of his worldly and vain spirit. **Between the Saints and those that are full of the spirit of vanity, there are some similarities. Both are guided with power and confidence by a spirit**. Some to the Kingdom of Heaven, while the others to hell, to forgetfulness and denial of Jesus Christ and The Kingdom of Heaven.

Three types of people

Saint Nikita Stithatos divides people in three categories: "The Holy Scripture acknowledges three states of life: bodily, souled and spiritually. **The bodily** state is dedicate entirely to pleasures and joys of the present life and has nothing to do with the souled state, neither the spiritual life, even if it would intend to grasp something from those. **The souled one is somehow in the middle**, between sin and virtue and seeks to take care and fortify the body as well as to receive boast from other people. It also forsakes the labours of virtue and run to bodily deeds. It does not join to the virtue, for its harshness and effort, and does not fight against the sin in order not to lose the people's boasts. Finally, the spiritual state doesn't want to have nothing in common with the two states already mentioned and to descend towards either of them as they are both evil."

Blessed Theophylact of Ochrid expressed a similar opinion: "There are three settlements: the bodily, the souled and the spiritually. ...**when someone is carried on the Holy Spirit** and no longer lives himself but Christ lives within, **then he is spiritual**."

Therefore, there are three categories of people on Earth: bodies, souls, and spirits – those full of the grace of the Holy Spirit. Just as an empty bottle is called bottle and when it is full of wine we say, "bring the wine", and we think at the wine from the bottle not at the bottle. In the same way, if the Holy Spirit is in the soul, we say that man is spirit, as the Spirit is what is most valuable in him. The Holy Scripture calls the people with a dead soul, flesh: "*My Spirit shall not strive with man forever, for he is indeed flash*" (Genesis. 6, 3). Man is more than often called soul, as the soul is the most valuable in him. But when the Holy Spirit dwells in his heart and he says along with the Apostle: "*It is no longer I who live, but Christ lives in me*" (Galatians 2, 20), they are called spirits (or spiritual). They are called spirits (when somebody is carried on the Spirit) according to what is the most important in them (the grace of Holy Spirit). The Holy Fathers explain that what the soul is for body, the Holy Spirit is for the soul. The very same person may be at a time body, then soul, and then spirit, may drive away grace and become again soul, and yet again, may acquire the grace and become again spirit or may suffer such a fall that he will become a body again and then, through repentance, soul, and by the great grace of God, a spirit again.

Saint John of Kronstadt writes: "I am sometimes flesh, sometimes soul and sometimes spirit."

Saint Theophan the Recluse adds: "So, man may be either spiritually – with rules, feelings and spiritual principles - or souled – with ideas, rules and soul feelings –or bodily with thoughts, matters and bodily feelings. This does not mean that when the man is spiritual, the souled and bodily have no place within, but the fact that the Spirit is the leader and the soul and body are ruled by the Spirit. It is not correct to say that when man is souled, the spiritual side and the bodily side no more exist. Therefore, in any state of life anyone might be, **always is possible the change from one state into another**, to get weaker a state in order to strengthen another one.""

Saint John of Kronstadt says: "The carnal man's entire life and occupations have a carnal tendency and carnal aim; his prayer is carnal, his learning and his teaching of others are carnal, his writings are carnal; at every step, in nearly every word, the carnal life appears. The carnal life manifests itself especially in everything relating to the man's appetites: here is the very seat of the carnal man. In proportion as the man by God's grace lays aside the carnal life, he begins to trample his carnal appetites under foot--he alters his food, ceases to live for insatiable appetite; gradually in his heart, faith, hope, and love begin to reign. Instead of eating, drinking, dress, riches, God, the soul, eternal life, eternal torment, occupy his thoughts and imagination. Instead of the love of money, of food, drink, dress, the luxury of his house and surroundings, love for God, for men, a longing to dwell with the Angels and Saints; instead of food and drink, hunger and thirst, and the diligent reading and listening to the Word of God and Divine service.

"Previously his enemies were those who hindered his outward well-being, now he bears privations with equanimity; previously he slept much and found pleasure in sleep, now he sleeps little and intentionally deprives himself of sweet sleep; previously he gratified the flesh in every way, now he mortifies it so that it may not rebel against the spirit."

Chapter 5

The Inner Seal

The Christian's Seal is The Holy Spirit

When will be the end of the world? It's not wrong to examine the signs so that it does not catch you unexpectedly, as Theophan the Recluse says: "Death is yet expected by one or another; but God's day by no one...But isn't better to wait it, so that we would not be caught unprepared?"

The Romanian Saint Callinicus of Cernica was concerned about this and thought that the end of the world will come during his lifetime. And he no longer wanted to build a new church in his monastery. But Saint George and Saint Nicholas were shown to him and told him to build the church as the end will be in the year of 1992. Meaning that, from then on will start to reveal the events of the end of the world.

Other Saints also pointed to the year of 1992 as the beginning of the end (Saint Niphon of Constantia the Wonderworker). It is, therefore, very probable that we live in the latest times, when many of the events of the end start to happen around us.

Thus, if it is true that we are getting closer to the end of the world, that means that the time of the final sealing is getting closer.

Many are concerned not to be sealed but without going more often to the church, without taking care of their souls or at least leaving the heavy sins. Thus, they are demonstrating disregard, not only in the issue of salvation, but also of sealing.

The issue of outside seal seems to be a true global issue that worries alike Catholics, Protestants, Orthodox, atheists, yogis, and so on. But, the issue of **inside seal** is only ours, an issue of the Orthodox.

The Christians' seal is, as the Church says, the Holy Spirit, and the others' seal is also a spirit, but the spirit of vanity, the worldly spirit, the Antichrist spirit. Holy Apostle Paul points writes: *"God also has sealed us and given us the Spirit in our hearts"* (2 Corinthians 1, 22) and the same is said at the baptism service. *"For as many as are lead by the Spirit of God, these are sons of God.* (Romans 8, 14)". *"If anyone does not have the Spirit of Christ, he is not His"* (Romans, 8, 9).

The Christians' seal is the Holy Spirit, while the Antichrist seal is the worldly spirit. Saint Ignatius Brianchaninov says: "Just as their spirit is in a state of enmity to Christ, in the same extent it is in a state of communion with Antichrist. **Those leaded by the spirit of Antichrist forsake Christ,** they accepted the Antichrist in their spirit, started the communion with Antichrist and worshipped to him in spirit, recognizing him as their god. *And for this reason God will send them strong delusion, that they should believe the lie, that they all may be condemned they who did not believe the truth but had pleasure in unrighteousness"* (2 Thessalonians 2, 11-12). "The reason why the Jewish forsake The Saviour was their immoral life, both private and social, which was nothing else than a constant infringement of God's Law. Let's chase away all reasons for forsaken so that we do not fall into forsaken. *As many times the sinner agrees with sin with which he is in communion,* says Tikhon of Zadonsk *as many times he forsakes Christ from his heart. And how many times he fulfils the sin with his deeds as many times he worships to the idol.* **To live incessantly in sin equals to constantly forsake Christ,** even if such a fact was not uttered with a loud voice. But, ah! It has already been uttered, it was uttered a long time ago. Tongue and lips cannot not to reveal the forsaking and the mysterious apostasy of the heart: both seem to speak unwillingly."

The Inside Seal foreruns the Outside Seal

We cannot speak of the final, outside seal if we do not speak first about the inside, spiritual seal. The outside seal is the final stage when almost all people will be already sealed by their own way of life and filled and enlivened by the spirit of vanity. **The inside seal foreruns the outside seal.**

We must rely on the inside work, so we will grow also in the outside ones. We must lay the foundation on the rock, not on the sand (Matthew 7, 24-27). Saint John Chrysostom says: "The Lord names *rock* the strength of His teachings. His commandments are stronger than rock and rise above the waves whoever fulfils them. The one who firmly guards them does not conquer only the people who fight him, but also the demons that conspire against him." On the other hand, he says: "When He spoke about what defiles man and what does not defile man, Christ distinguishes between what is clean and what is unclean and necessarily shows that **inside cleanliness is followed by the outside cleanliness. The contrary is impossible**."

Meanwhile, having faith and hope in God, we know that we will receive power to overcome this temptation, just as any other temptation. Temptation is not beyond our powers: *God will not allow you to be tempted beyond what you are able* (1 Corinthians 10, 13). This will also be valid during the final seal. Therefore, the Christians who will want to and will endeavour, will defeat. No matter how *without escape* may seem the trap that lies all around us, it will crack in many places and finally will collapse in their entirety. Antichrist plan will have many fissures when it will be put into practice. Only God's work can be perfect. Walking the path shown by God, we can only be winners even if, from the outside, according to the world standard, we will seem opposite.

The outside seal will be connected to science, culture, and technology. The seal itself will probably be presented as a participation in a great scientific experiment and as an act of culture. And those who used to give priority to science and technology in their lives, by virtue of habit, will get this seal without any resistance.

Trusting in science absolutely and worshipping human culture, they are already apostates. Even if they get rid of the outside seal, they have anyway the inside seal.

The Orthodox Church knows that the Christians' **seal** is the **grace of the Holy Spirit**. While the others' seal is also a spirit, but the spirit of the world. The spirit of the world is built and mixed with science and worldly culture.

Just as the aboriginals from Central America were deceived with pieces of coloured glass and different kinds of tinsel so that they can take their gold, the Christians of the end are also deceived with devices with coloured lights, video sequences, music and shows and other like this to kidnap and replace with "something else" their faith, hope, and love of God.

Even if Saint John the Evangelist would not have written in the Book of *Revelation* about the seal of Antichrist, still, a part of the true Christians would have escaped the seal. How would they escape? They would have escaped being guided and advised by the Gospel commands. They would have followed poverty and left behind the places full of wealth; they would have sought peace and stepped away from everything troubling them; they would have sought piety and exited just as from Egypt, away from the places where vanity rules and works.

Saint John the Evangelist talks about seal in The Book of *Revelation* because God wants to draw out and save as many people as possible. When the end will be near, there will be more and more help for those willing to save themselves, just for saving as many people as possible. *But when you are tempted, he will also provide a way out so that you can endure it* (1 Corinthians 10, 13).

Even if the situation may seem extremely heavy, finally, God will give salvation that will seem so marvellous for His friends and even more devastating for His enemies. Amen!

Made in the USA
Las Vegas, NV
08 November 2023

80465637R00062